FREEZE

Super-nourishing meals to
batch cook, freeze and
eat on demand

FREEZE

BY ✕ RUBY

Ruby Bell and Milly Bagot

MITCHELL BEAZLEY

To Julia and Finns, where it all began.

First published in Great Britain in 2021 by Mitchell Beazley, a division of
Octopus Publishing Group Ltd, Carmelite House, 50 Victoria Embankment,
London EC4Y 0DZ

www.octopusbooks.co.uk
www.octopusbooksusa.com

An Hachette UK Company
www.hachette.co.uk

Distributed in the US by Hachette Book Group, 1290 Avenue of the Americas,
4th and 5th Floors, New York, NY 10104

Distributed in Canada by Canadian Manda Group, 664 Annette St., Toronto,
Ontario, Canada M6S 2C8

978-1-784-72748-2

A CIP catalogue record for this book is available from the British Library.

Printed and bound in China.

10 9 8 7 6 5 4 3 2 1

Recipe notes

The timings given for reheating in the microwave are based on using an
850-watt oven on high (full power).

If using a conventional oven, increase the temperature by 20°C (i.e. if a recipe
gives a temperature of 180°C fan, increase it to 200°C for a conventional oven).

Editorial Director: Eleanor Maxfield
Art Director: Juliette Norsworthy
Senior Editor: Leanne Bryan
Copy Editor: Jo Richardson
Designer: Lizzie Ballantyne
Photographer: Haarala Hamilton Photography
Food Stylist: Becks Wilkinson
Props Stylist: Rachel Vere
Production Manager: Caroline Alberti

Contents

Introduction

Wouldn't it be nice to open your freezer to find a carefully curated stash of nourishing and delicious meals ready to heat up in a jiffy? We recognized that the home freezer is all too often underused, containing only a packet of fish fingers and a bag of peas, maybe a tray of ice or a supermarket-bought pizza. So we founded ByRuby to change people's perceptions of frozen food. Enter the 'Freezer of the Future' – a way of preserving nature's best. Think of it like 'pressing pause' on a fresh dish that is packed with nutrients until you decide to 'press play' and reap the benefits when you are ready for a quality midweek meal or a weekend feast.

When we first started, we tested and tweaked to create wholesome, all-natural dishes that taste just as good when cooked from frozen as freshly made. Once we had nailed the recipes, we began delivering our frozen meals directly to food-loving folk across the UK. Stocking people's freezers with family favourites such as fish pie, through to more unusual freezer-friendly dishes like miso ramen, has proved to our customers that frozen really can be best, judging by the hugely positive feedback we have had from them. So now it's your turn to give our recipes a go. Like our frozen food, this selection of recipes is seriously special and very close to our hearts.

Our lives are getting ever busier and yet we know that decent, nourishing food is the basis of a healthy and happy life. Batch cooking for freezing not only saves time but is economical financially too. Whether you are living on your own or have a large family to feed, or are in need of a quick, energizing lunch at home or at work, a delicious dinner after a busy day or impressive make-ahead dishes for effortlessly entertaining friends, you can relax knowing that you only have to reach for just what's required from your new best friend – the freezer!

Ingredients

We strongly believe that you should buy the best ingredients you can afford. You will very rarely waste anything if you use your freezer efficiently, so sourcing premium produce might even save you money once you get into the swing of batch cooking and freezing.

As a basis for sustainable living, this book is packed full of delicious vegetarian and vegan recipes featuring vegetables, grains and pulses. These ingredients should be just as high in quality as any meat and fish used in the other recipes, ensuring that plant-based meals are equally as tasty.

All the ingredients used in this book should be easy to find at your local supermarket. We love shopping seasonally, so if a recipe calls for broccoli but it is asparagus season, asparagus can be substituted for a lovely treat. Likewise, if you can't find hake, use a different white fish, or swap trout for salmon or another oily fish. And you can usually substitute beef for lamb or pork or the other way round. Dried Puy lentils or beans work really well instead of any stewing or braising meat if cooked for the appropriate time. Our recipes are designed to be flexible, as we hate the idea of wastage, and so we encourage you to use what you have and be creative.

It is worth noting that frozen raw ingredients such as meat, fish or vegetables are perfectly safe to use instead of fresh and are equal in quality in many cases. Just make sure that any frozen raw ingredients you are using are defrosted (except where peas and some other veg are added frozen during the cooking process), then fully cooked as directed in our recipes before freezing the finished dish. In recipes where fresh fish is frozen raw, such as in Roasted Salmon with Braised Puy Lentils (see page 55), you can swap the fresh fish for frozen once the lentils have cooled and return to the freezer.

Try if you can to use ingredients in peak condition, when they are really fresh or fully ripe, to enjoy them at their best in terms of taste and nutritional value.

Equipment

Standard kitchen equipment is all that is needed for the recipes in this book, but the following items are worth highlighting as essential or very helpful:

- Kitchen scales
- Large heavy-based pan with a lid
- Food processor
- Hand blender or freestanding blender
- Electric hand mixer (if making sweet treats)
- Plenty of freezer-safe containers (see right)

Freezing

Making a large quantity of a dish doesn't take much more time than cooking for one or two, and dividing it up into portions for freezing means you will have a dependable supply of quality meals to hand in your freezer.

It is a very satisfying job to get your freezer in good order in anticipation of a well-stocked treasure trove of delicious dishes. Make sure it is thoroughly clean, and if there is a build-up of ice, defrost it.

Always ensure food is cooled completely before freezing. Assemble a good selection of freezer-safe containers, which should all be airtight, or wrap tightly in clingfilm or foil. Appropriate foods can also be wrapped directly in clingfilm or foil. Also bear in mind your preferred reheating method when portioning and freezing your food (see page 9).

Freezing for the microwave

Microwave-safe plastic storage containers, ramekins and other ovenproof ceramic or earthenware dishes and Pyrex containers are all perfect for reheating in the microwave. If in doubt, check the bottom of any container or dish and it should state if it is safe to use in the microwave. Always wrap containers without neatly fitting lids (or anything you are wrapping directly) tightly in clingfilm and be sure to pierce the clingfilm before reheating in the microwave.

Freezer bags are an excellent and space-efficient way to store casseroles, sauces and even finger foods, such as our Cornflake Chicken Dippers (see page 93) and Fishcakes (see page 94). You will need to defrost anything liquid before heating if you freeze directly into freezer bags; always make sure you do so in a bowl or on an appropriately sized plate to avoid any nasty surprises if the seal pops open. Choose freezer bags with hardy seals rather than tie handles.

You can freeze purées for babies, or certain sauces in ice-cube trays (see the individual recipes for details) and then pop the cubes out directly into a freezer bag for later use. When reheating, transfer the frozen cubes to a microwave-safe container and heat as directed in the recipes (alternatively, they can be reheated in a pan on the hob). Never use foil or any kind of metal or enamelware in the microwave.

Freezing for the oven

Disposable foil containers, Pyrex containers, enamelware, ramekins and other ovenproof ceramic or earthenware dishes work really well for storing in the freezer and then reheating directly in the oven. Most modern dishes will state if they are ovenproof on the bottom. Always wrap tightly in clingfilm or foil to avoid freezer burn and make sure you remove the clingfilm, or any lid, before reheating in the oven, and replace with foil if directed to do so in the recipe.

Portioning

We have suggested how many portions each recipe will make, so simply divide up the finished dish evenly according to the portion number specified.

Labelling & dating

Make sure you label your food clearly and firmly with the date you cooked it and a best before date (see below). It is important to keep a track of your freezer contents and rotate as necessary, bringing older batches of food to the top or front of the freezer so that you don't find any nasty surprises lurking at the bottom or back in a year's time.

The ideal temperature to store frozen food is -18°C (-0.4°F) and almost all of our recipes are best kept for up to about six months at this temperature. If your freezer isn't as cold as that, the food will keep in optimum condition for a shorter period of time.

Reheating

The majority of our recipes reheat very successfully directly from the freezer in the microwave or oven. Each recipe has suggested reheating instructions, but do bear in mind that microwaves and ovens vary, so use these as a guide, not gospel. The timings given for reheating in the microwave are based on using an 850-watt oven on high (full power). If you freeze a larger quantity of a recipe in one batch, more than two portions' worth, it is best to defrost the food before reheating.

Reheating on the hob

Some recipes can be reheated on the hob directly from the freezer – in particular anything that has been frozen in ice-cube trays for babies. It is important to use a low heat and keep a close eye, stirring regularly.

Flavour

Most dishes taste pretty much the same after freezing and many actually improve and intensify in flavour with freezing. We find that for slow-cooked dishes freezing is like a very long and slow marination process, with the flavours permeating meats in particular even more effectively.

Sometimes stringent flavours like lemon can lessen slightly during the freezing process. If you are lemon nuts like us, it is worth adding an extra spritz where lemon juice is called for in a recipe.

Catering for children

We love cooking for kids at ByRuby, and Milly's children are our perfect taste testers. Family Food (from 6 Months) on page 91 is a really useful section catering for all ages. The recipes avoid extra seasoning for babies and young children, but indicate where you can add seasoning and sometimes extra spice for grown-ups. If you cook any of our other recipes for babies or children, try to avoid additional salt in cooking.

Ruby – how frozen helped me

After a full-on day in the kitchen, the last thing I want to do is cook another meal. It's hard to juggle eating well with a busy lifestyle, although that's really important to my husband and me. Even foodies sometimes don't have time to cook every day! I found that the other convenient alternatives are often very low quality, unhealthy and expensive. When I started developing frozen food, I realized that it really is better than fresh. I can come home now, put one of our handmade, all-natural meals in the oven, take a bath and then dinner is ready. I can relax knowing exactly what's in my food. It really has made that midweek nightmare into a midweek wonder. The freezer is my friend and I will never look back.

Milly – how frozen helped me

When I was pregnant with my first baby, my sisters filled my freezer in anticipation of the new bundle and it was the best present I could have been given. Having a nourishing and tasty meal ready to pop in the oven when I was sleep deprived and exhausted was such

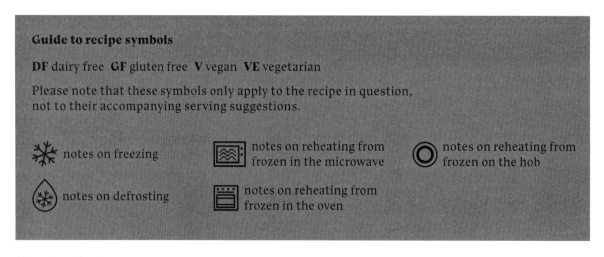

Guide to recipe symbols

DF dairy free **GF** gluten free **V** vegan **VE** vegetarian

Please note that these symbols only apply to the recipe in question, not to their accompanying serving suggestions.

notes on freezing

notes on reheating from frozen in the microwave

notes on reheating from frozen on the hob

notes on defrosting

notes on reheating from frozen in the oven

Ruby (left) and Milly (right)

a relief. It allowed me to take some time out, have a bath, read a book or put my feet up when the last thing I wanted to do was cook. My love of the freezer has continued into my lifestyle raising three children. I always batch cook – cooking eight portions really doesn't take much more time than cooking two – or have a good selection of our ByRuby

meals in the freezer. From weaning through to childhood, not to mention adulthood, having a well-stocked freezer is such a comfort. There is always a quick and wholesome lunch or dinner to hand, and the children always have something tasty and nourishing whether I am there or not. I hope you learn to love the freezer as much as I do!

Easy midweek meals

5-a-day udon noodles

The clue is in the title... This recipe is packed full of vegetables, super healthy and nourishing, and one of the most popular dishes on our website. The veg we use are only suggestions – any seasonal veg would work brilliantly here.

Makes 4–5 portions **DF / V / VE**

2 tablespoons sesame oil
20g (¾oz) fresh root ginger, peeled and
    finely chopped
1 tablespoon crushed garlic
1 tablespoon chopped deseeded red chilli
3 tablespoons teriyaki sauce
3 tablespoons dark soy sauce
1 tablespoon lime juice
1 tablespoon rice wine vinegar
200g (7oz) tofu, cut into 2cm (¾-inch)
    squares
1 head of broccoli, cut into florets
olive oil
30g (1oz) cashew nuts
200g (7oz) Chinese cabbage or seasonal
    leafy greens, sliced
100g (3½oz) chestnut mushrooms,
    finely sliced
100g (3½oz) frozen or fresh edamame
    beans
100g (3½oz) spring onions, finely chopped
400g (14oz) precooked udon noodles
salt and pepper

To garnish (optional):
1 tablespoon sesame seeds
30g (1oz) fresh coriander, chopped
lime wedges

1 Preheat the oven to 180°C fan (400°F), Gas Mark 6. Line two baking trays with nonstick baking paper.

2 Heat a nonstick frying pan over a medium heat. Add the sesame oil and then the ginger, garlic and chilli and cook for 5 minutes, stirring occasionally.

3 Add the teriyaki and soy sauces, lime juice and vinegar and cook for about 5 minutes until reduced to a coating consistency. Stir in the tofu and cook for about 10 minutes until golden.

4 Meanwhile, spread the broccoli florets out on one lined baking tray, sprinkle with salt and drizzle with olive oil. Roast for about 10 minutes until slightly golden and charred around the edges.

5 While the broccoli is roasting, toast the cashew nuts on the other lined baking tray for about 5 minutes until golden. Leave to cool, then roughly chop.

6 Add all the remaining ingredients to the frying pan and cook for about 5 minutes until the greens and noodles are tender. Then stir through the roasted nuts and broccoli and season to taste.

7 Serve sprinkled with sesame seeds and coriander and with extra lime wedges to garnish, if you like.

❄️ Portion out the noodle mixture into appropriate containers (see pages 8–9). Leave to cool, then seal, label and date (see page 9) before freezing.

〰️ Microwave on high for 3 minutes, then remove from the microwave and stir. Re-cover but don't seal and microwave for a further 5 minutes or until piping hot. Leave to stand for 3 minutes before serving.

▦ Preheat the oven to 160°C fan (350°F), Gas Mark 4. Uncover the ovenproof container and then cover the top with foil. Place on a baking sheet in the centre of the oven for 40–45 minutes or until piping hot. Leave to stand for 3 minutes before serving.

Chicken wholefood bowl

Nutritious and satisfying, this recipe offers everything you need in one meal, making it ideal for a quick lunch. You can swap the squash and beetroots for whatever roasting veg are in season (see page 31 for some alternatives).

Makes 8-10 portions **DF** (if using homemade pesto made with nutritional yeast flakes) / **GF**

1 small butternut squash, about 400g (14oz), peeled, deseeded and cut into 2cm (¾-inch) cubes
6 medium beetroots, about 400g (14oz), scrubbed and sliced and/or cut into 2cm (¾-inch) cubes
vegetable oil
250g (9oz) quinoa, well rinsed and drained
grated zest and juice of 1 lemon
½ quantity of Best-ever Pesto (see page 140), or 60g (2¼oz) ready-made pesto
1 medium chicken, about 1.5kg (3lb 5oz), roasted (see page 149), or leftover roast chicken, meat removed from the bone, skinned and shredded, about 500g (1lb 2oz) (reserve the carcass and/or bones for freezing and making stock – see page 149)
1 bag of chopped curly kale, about 150g (5½oz)
2 tablespoons olive oil
250g (9oz) cherry tomatoes, halved
15g (½oz) flat leaf parsley, leaves picked and chopped
salt
3 tablespoons sunflower seeds, to garnish (optional)

1 Preheat the oven to 180°C fan (400°F), Gas Mark 6.

2 Spread the butternut squash and beetroot cubes out on two large baking trays and drizzle with vegetable oil. Roast for 20–25 minutes or until cooked through and slightly caramelized.

3 Meanwhile, put the quinoa into a pan, cover with water and bring to the boil. Reduce the heat and simmer for about 15 minutes, stirring occasionally, until just cooked through. Drain, put into a bowl and stir through the lemon zest and juice.

4 Mix the pesto through the shredded roast chicken.

5 Drizzle the kale with the olive oil and massage with your hands until soft. Season with salt, then fold through the tomatoes.

6 Stir the chopped parsley through the roasted vegetables.

7 To assemble, arrange the pesto chicken, quinoa, roasted veg and finally the kale and tomato mixture in each serving bowl. Sprinkle with the sunflower seeds to garnish, if you like.

❄ Portion out the pesto chicken, quinoa, roasted veg, and kale and tomato mixture into appropriate containers (see pages 8–9) and leave to cool. Seal, label and date (see page 9) before freezing.

Microwave on high for 3 minutes, then remove from the microwave and stir. Re-cover but don't seal and microwave for a further 5 minutes or until piping hot. Leave to stand for 3 minutes before serving.

Preheat the oven to 160°C fan (350°F), Gas Mark 4. Uncover the ovenproof container and then cover the top with foil. Place on a baking sheet in the centre of the oven for 40–45 minutes or until piping hot. Leave to stand for 3 minutes before serving.

Ruby's one-pot bean chilli

This is such a versatile recipe – great with a baked potato, wholewheat pasta or as it comes with some coconut yogurt and freshly chopped avocado. It also makes a great vegan taco and wrap filling. I use a can of black beans here, but you can use any kind you may have or prefer.

Makes 6–7 portions **DF / GF / V / VE**

vegetable oil
1 large onion, finely chopped
3 garlic cloves, crushed
2cm (¾-inch) piece of fresh root ginger, peeled and finely chopped
2 red chillies, deseeded and finely sliced
½ teaspoon chilli powder
2 teaspoons cumin seeds, crushed
2 tablespoons harissa
½ tablespoon cacao powder
180g (6¼oz) dried Puy lentils, well rinsed and drained
120g (4¼oz) quinoa, well rinsed and drained
400g (14oz) can chopped tomatoes
800ml (1½ pints) vegetable stock
400g (14oz) can beans, such as black beans, drained and rinsed
salt and pepper
15g (½oz) fresh coriander sprigs, to garnish (optional)

To serve (optional):
coconut yogurt
freshly chopped avocado

1 Heat a large, heavy-based pan over a medium heat. Add a glug of vegetable oil and then the onion, garlic and ginger and cook for 5 minutes.

2 Stir in the red chillies, chilli powder, cumin seeds, harissa and cacao powder and cook for a further 5 minutes.

3 Add the lentils and quinoa, then pour over the tomatoes and stock. Bring to a simmer and cook over a low heat for about 20 minutes, until the lentils and quinoa are cooked through, stirring occasionally and adding a little water if needed.

4 Stir in the beans and heat through for a few minutes.

5 Remove from the heat and season to taste, garnish with the coriander, if using, and serve with a dollop of coconut yogurt and some freshly chopped avocado, if you like.

❄ Portion out the bean chilli into appropriate containers (see pages 8–9). Leave to cool, then seal, label and date (see page 9) before freezing.

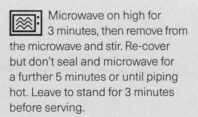 Microwave on high for 3 minutes, then remove from the microwave and stir. Re-cover but don't seal and microwave for a further 5 minutes or until piping hot. Leave to stand for 3 minutes before serving.

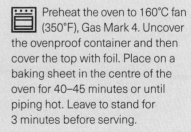 Preheat the oven to 160°C fan (350°F), Gas Mark 4. Uncover the ovenproof container and then cover the top with foil. Place on a baking sheet in the centre of the oven for 40–45 minutes or until piping hot. Leave to stand for 3 minutes before serving.

Keralan vegetable curry

I was lucky enough to be given this recipe by a lady in Kerala who was cooking it on a street stall – the aroma was intoxicating. Serve this curry with our Fail-safe Mixed Rice with Parsley and homemade Naan Breads (see pages 134 and 148).

Makes 5 portions **DF / GF / V / VE**

vegetable oil
1½ tablespoons black mustard seeds
15 fresh curry leaves
100g (3½oz) desiccated coconut, soaked in
    200ml (7fl oz) hot water for 20 minutes
2 × 400ml (14fl oz) cans coconut milk
4 tablespoons cashew nuts, soaked in
    100ml (3½fl oz) hot water for 20 minutes
6 large potatoes, peeled and cut into 2cm
    (¾-inch) cubes
4 aubergines, cut into 2cm (¾-inch) cubes
1 large cauliflower, cut into 2cm (¾-inch)
    cubes, inner leaves retained
2 teaspoons ground turmeric
grated zest and juice of 1 lime
16g (½oz) fresh coriander, leaves picked
    and chopped (optional)
salt

For the curry paste:
2 large onions, roughly chopped
4 red chillies, deseeded and chopped
3cm (1¼-inch) piece of fresh root ginger,
    peeled and roughly chopped
4 garlic cloves, roughly chopped
2 tablespoons cumin seeds, lightly crushed
2 tablespoons ground turmeric
2 tablespoons ground coriander

1 Put all the curry paste ingredients into a food processor and blitz to a paste, adding a little water as necessary. Alternatively, use a hand blender.

2 Heat a large, heavy-based pan over a low heat. Add 3 tablespoons of vegetable oil and then the mustard seeds and curry leaves and toast for about 3–5 minutes until aromatic.

3 Stir in the curry paste along with 1 teaspoon of salt and cook for 10 minutes, stirring frequently.

4 Add the coconut with its soaking water and cook for a further 5 minutes, then pour in the coconut milk.

5 Blitz the cashew nuts and their soaking water in a food processor until smooth. Then add to the curry sauce, reduce the heat and simmer gently for about 30 minutes, stirring occasionally, until the sauce has thickened.

6 Meanwhile, preheat the oven to 180°C fan (400°F), Gas Mark 6.

7 Spread the vegetables out on two baking trays. Sprinkle with the turmeric, season with salt and drizzle with vegetable oil, then roast for 20–30 minutes or until cooked through.

8 Stir the roasted vegetables into the curry sauce, then remove from the heat and add the lime zest and juice and coriander, if using.

Portion out the curry mixture into appropriate containers (see pages 8–9). Leave to cool, then seal, label and date (see page 9) before freezing.

Microwave on high for 3 minutes, then remove from the microwave and stir. Re-cover but don't seal and microwave for a further 5 minutes or until piping hot. Leave to stand for 3 minutes before serving.

Preheat the oven to 160°C fan (350°F), Gas Mark 4. Uncover the ovenproof container and then cover the top with foil. Place on a baking sheet in the centre of the oven for 40–45 minutes or until piping hot. Leave to stand for 3 minutes before serving.

Thai green tofu, chicken or salmon
with seasonal vegetables

This is a great dish for using up veggies in your refrigerator or seasonal veg box, so feel free to substitute any you may have around for those listed. For a more substantial meal, serve with our Fail-safe Mixed Rice with Parsley (see page 134).

Makes 8–9 portions **DF** / **GF** / **V** and **VE** (if made with tofu and fish sauce omitted)

3 baby aubergines, cut into 4cm (1½-inch) cubes
vegetable oil
200g (7oz) new potatoes, halved
100g (3½oz) baby corn, halved
200g (7oz) green beans, halved
400g (14oz) firm tofu, cut into 2cm (¾-inch) cubes OR 4 boneless, skinless chicken thighs, cut into 2cm (¾-inch) chunks OR 2 skinless salmon fillets, about 200g (7oz) each, cut into 2cm (¾-inch) chunks
grated zest and juice of 1 lime
10g (¼oz) fresh coriander leaves, chopped
gluten-free dark soy sauce (optional)
salt
handful of Thai basil sprigs, to garnish

For the curry base:
2 tablespoons vegetable oil
2 garlic cloves, finely chopped
1½ tablespoons Thai green curry paste
4 fresh kaffir lime leaves
2 × 400ml (14fl oz) cans coconut milk
3 teaspoons fish sauce

1 Preheat the oven to 180°C fan (400°F), Gas Mark 6.

2 Spread the aubergine chunks out on a baking tray, drizzle with vegetable oil and roast for 15–20 minutes or until cooked through.

3 Meanwhile, make the curry base. Heat the vegetable oil in a wok or large frying pan over a medium heat. Add the garlic and stir-fry for 2 minutes, being careful not to burn it.

4 Add the curry paste and cook for 5 minutes, stirring constantly.

5 Stir in the lime leaves, coconut milk and fish sauce, reduce the heat and simmer gently for 10–15 minutes, stirring occasionally.

6 While the curry is simmering, bring a saucepan of well-salted water to the boil. Add the potatoes and cook for 5 minutes, then add the corn and beans and cook for 3 minutes. Drain.

7 If you are using tofu, place on a baking tray and roast for about 10 minutes until golden, then add to the curry sauce. If you are using chicken, add to the curry sauce and cook for 10–15 minutes or until cooked through and tender. If you are using salmon and eating now, add to the curry sauce and cook for 5 minutes or until just cooked through. If freezing, remove the curry sauce from the heat and just add the salmon to the sauce, as the reheating process will cook the salmon perfectly.

8 Stir all the cooked vegetables into the curry sauce and add the lime zest and juice and the coriander. Season to taste with soy sauce (if using) or salt.

9 Garnish with the Thai basil sprigs before serving.

Portion out the green curry mixture into appropriate containers (see pages 8–9). Leave to cool, then seal, label and date (see page 9) before freezing.

Microwave on high for 3 minutes, them remove from the microwave and stir. Re-cover but don't seal and microwave for a further 5 minutes or until piping hot. Leave to stand for 3 minutes before serving.

Preheat the oven to 160°C fan (350°F), Gas Mark 4. Uncover the ovenproof container and then cover the top with foil. Place on a baking sheet in the centre of the oven for 40–45 minutes or until piping hot. Leave to stand for 3 minutes before serving.

Asian chicken noodles

with courgette & carrot ribbons

This aromatic broth with chicken and lots of fragrant herbs takes me back to the street stalls of Thailand. One of the things I love most about Thailand is the food. The fast-food culture there is something entirely different to what we think of in the Western world. Huge vats of bubbling, fragrant broth ladled over noodles with pick-and-mix vegetables, meat and herbs. Chilli – and lots of it – salt, acidity, sweetness, aromatics... Having some broth in the freezer is always useful as it's so versatile and can be poured over leftover vegetables, meat or fish. A spritz of lime and some cooked noodles tossed in sesame oil and you have a quick and nourishing lunch, whenever you need it!

Makes 8–10 portions **DF**

100g (3½oz) dried rice noodles
1 courgette, shaved lengthways with a peeler or mandolin
1 carrot, shaved lengthways with a peeler or mandolin
1 pack of pak choi, about 250g (9oz), finely sliced
100g (3½oz) frozen or fresh edamame beans
1 small bag of baby spinach leaves, about 100g (3½oz)
½ bunch of spring onions, about 50g (1¾oz), finely sliced
15g (½oz) mint, finely chopped
15g (½oz) fresh coriander, leaves picked and chopped
1 medium chicken, about 1.5kg (3lb 5oz), roasted (see page 149), or leftover roast chicken, meat removed from the bone, skinned and shredded, about 500g (1lb 2oz) (reserve the carcass and/or bones for freezing and making stock – see page 149)
½ tablespoon sesame oil
salt

1 For the broth, heat a large pan over a medium heat. Add a little vegetable oil and then the ginger and garlic and cook for 3 minutes.

2 Add the stock, tom yum paste, lime leaves, sugar, fish and soy sauces and mirin, bring to a simmer and cook for 10 minutes, stirring occasionally.

3 Meanwhile, soak the noodles in boiling water for 3–5 minutes or until starting to soften, stirring occasionally, then drain.

4 Remove the pan from the heat and add the lime juice.

5 Combine the prepared vegetables, herbs and cooked chicken in a bowl, then drizzle with the sesame oil and season to taste with salt.

6 To serve, portion out the noodles into bowls, top with the vegetable and chicken mixture, then pour over the hot broth.

For the broth:
vegetable oil
45g (1½oz) fresh root ginger, peeled
    and finely diced
1 tablespoon finely chopped garlic
1 litre (1¾ pints) chicken stock
50g (1¾oz) tom yum paste
6 fresh kaffir lime leaves
1 teaspoon sugar
1 tablespoon fish sauce
1 tablespoon gluten-free dark soy sauce
½ tablespoon mirin
juice of 1 lime

❄ Portion out the noodles followed by the vegetable and chicken mixture into appropriate containers (see pages 8–9), then pour over the broth. Leave to cool, then seal, label and date (see page 9) before freezing.

Microwave on high for 3 minutes, then remove from the microwave and stir. Re-cover but don't seal and microwave for a further 5 minutes or until piping hot. Leave to stand for 3 minutes before serving.

Preheat the oven to 160°C fan (350°F), Gas Mark 4. Uncover the ovenproof container and then cover the top with foil. Place on a baking sheet in the centre of the oven for 40–45 minutes or until piping hot. Leave to stand for 3 minutes before serving.

Fish of the day
with supergrains & salsa verde

This dish is one of my ultimate favourites, which I often batch cook and have for lunch when I'm working from home. Oily fish works best when reheated from frozen, such as salmon, trout and mackerel, but cod or hake would also work well here, so see what your fishmonger has in fresh. The fragrant and punchy salsa verde makes a great addition to the freezer on its own – you can double the recipe and freeze the extra batch in ice-cube trays to defrost as needed (see page 141).

Makes 8 portions **DF / GF**

olive oil
250g (9oz) leeks, trimmed, cleaned and
    finely chopped
250g (9oz) baby spinach leaves
200g (7oz) frozen peas
10g (¼oz) flat leaf parsley, leaves picked
    and chopped
grated zest and juice of 1 lemon
3 tablespoons olive oil
200g (7oz) quinoa, cooked and drained
    (see page 133)
150g (5½oz) wild rice or black rice, cooked
    and drained (see page 134)
1 quantity of Salsa Verde (see page 141)
800g (1lb 12oz) piece of skinless fish fillet,
    cut into pieces about 100g (3½oz) each
salt and pepper

1 Heat a pan over a medium heat. Add a little olive oil and then the leeks and sweat for about 5 minutes until soft and translucent.

2 Stir the spinach into the leeks, then remove the pan from the heat and stir in the peas and parsley. Season to taste.

3 Meanwhile, if eating now, preheat the oven to 180°C fan (400°F), Gas Mark 6 for cooking the fish.

4 Stir the lemon zest and juice and olive oil through the cooked quinoa and wild or black rice, and season to taste.

5 Spread the salsa verde over the fish fillets. If freezing, keep the fish raw, but otherwise place on a baking tray and bake for 6–8 minutes or until cooked to your liking.

6 Serve the fish on top of the grains and alongside the spinach and leek mixture.

❄️ Portion out the grains and the spinach and leek mixture into appropriate containers (see pages 8–9). Leave to cool, then top each portion with a salsa verde-dressed uncooked fish fillet. Seal, label and date (see page 9) before freezing.

〰️ Microwave on high for 3 minutes, then remove from the microwave, uncover and agitate the container gently from side to side. Re-cover but don't seal and microwave for a further 3 minutes or until piping hot. Leave to stand for 3 minutes before serving.

🔲 Preheat the oven to 160°C fan (350°F), Gas Mark 4. Uncover the ovenproof container and then cover the top with foil. Place on a baking sheet in the centre of the oven for 30–35 minutes or until piping hot. Leave to stand for 3 minutes before serving.

Roasted butternut squash & spinach dhal

This dish goes well with any of the other curries in the book. And the beauty of batch cooking is that you can grab a portion of each straight from the freezer for a flexible and convenient curry night feast! Just serve with chapattis and rice.

Makes 5–6 portions **DF / GF / V / VE**

vegetable oil
1 onion, finely chopped
3 garlic cloves, crushed
3cm (1¼-inch) piece of fresh root ginger,
   peeled and finely chopped
500g (1lb 2oz) dried red lentils, well rinsed
   and drained
2 × 400ml (14fl oz) cans coconut milk
500ml (18fl oz) water
1 butternut squash, peeled, deseeded and
   cut into about 2cm (¾-inch) cubes
150g (5½oz) fresh or frozen spinach leaves
grated zest and juice of 1 lime
grated zest and juice of ½ lemon
15g (½oz) fresh coriander, chopped, plus
   extra sprigs (optional) to garnish
salt
toasted coconut flakes, to garnish (optional)

For the spice mix:
1½ tablespoons cumin seeds
1 tablespoon fennel seeds
1 tablespoon coriander seeds
1 tablespoon ground turmeric
½ tablespoon garam masala
½ tablespoon ground cinnamon
½ teaspoon chilli powder
1 tablespoon black mustard seeds

1 To make the spice mix, put all the spices except the mustard seeds into a spice grinder and grind to a powder, or use a pestle and mortar. Then stir in the whole mustard seeds.

2 Heat a large, heavy-based pan over a medium heat, add the spice mix and toast for about 3–4 minutes until aromatic.

3 Add 2 tablespoons of vegetable oil and the onion and sweat for 5 minutes. Then add the garlic and ginger and cook for a further 5 minutes.

4 Stir in the lentils, followed by the coconut milk and measured water. Bring to a simmer, then reduce the heat to low and simmer gently for about 25–30 minutes, or until the lentils are cooked through, stirring occasionally and adding extra water if needed.

5 Meanwhile, preheat the oven to 180°C fan (400°F), Gas Mark 6.

6 Spread the squash cubes out on a baking tray, drizzle with vegetable oil and season with 1 teaspoon of salt. Roast for 20 minutes or until cooked through and slightly caramelized.

7 Stir the spinach into the curry along with the roasted squash. Remove from the heat and add the citrus zest and juice and the coriander. Adjust the seasoning to taste, then serve garnished with fresh coriander sprigs and toasted coconut flakes, if you like.

Portion out the dhal into appropriate containers (see pages 8–9). Leave to cool, then seal, label and date (see page 9) before freezing.

Microwave on high for 3 minutes, then remove from the microwave and stir. Re-cover but don't seal and microwave for a further 5 minutes or until piping hot. Leave to stand for 3 minutes before serving.

Preheat the oven to 160°C fan (350°F), Gas Mark 4. Uncover the ovenproof container and then cover the top with foil. Place on a baking sheet in the centre of the oven for 40–45 minutes or until piping hot. Leave to stand for 3 minutes before serving.

Vegetable & chickpea tagine

I love vegetable tagine. When I was younger and my parents had an allotment, we would always cook together and found that a tagine was the perfect way to use up any excess vegetables. So regard the vegetables listed here as a guideline only – any you might have in the refrigerator will work brilliantly.

Makes 5-6 portions **DF / GF / V / VE**

vegetable oil
4 red onions, cut into wedges
1 tablespoon crushed garlic
2 teaspoons ground cinnamon
2 teaspoons ground cumin
2 teaspoons chilli flakes
1 tablespoon harissa
1 tablespoon tomato purée
400g (14oz) can chopped tomatoes
500ml (18fl oz) vegetable stock
5 carrots, cut into 2cm (¾-inch) chunks
5 courgettes, cut into 2cm (¾-inch) chunks
2 aubergines, cut into 2cm (¾-inch) chunks
4 peppers (any colour or a mixture), cored, deseeded and cut into 2cm (¾-inch) chunks
250g (9oz) canned chickpeas, drained and rinsed
1 tablespoon cashew nuts
1 teaspoon ground turmeric
100g (3½oz) dried apricots, finely chopped
handful each of mint leaves, flat leaf parsley leaves and fresh coriander leaves, finely chopped
salt and pepper

1 Heat a large, heavy-based pan over a medium heat. Add a glug of vegetable oil and then the onions and garlic and sweat for about 10 minutes until the onions are translucent.

2 Stir in all the spices and the harissa and cook for 5 minutes, stirring frequently.

3 Add the tomato purée and tomatoes and stir well, then pour in the stock. Bring to a simmer, then reduce the heat and simmer gently for about 35 minutes, stirring occasionally, until the sauce is thick and rich.

4 Meanwhile, preheat the oven to 180°C fan (400°F), Gas Mark 6. Line three baking trays with nonstick baking paper.

5 Spread the carrot, courgette, aubergine and pepper chunks out on two lined baking trays, drizzle with vegetable oil and roast for 20 minutes or until cooked through.

6 Pat the chickpeas dry, spread out on the remaining lined baking tray and roast along with the vegetables for 10 minutes or until golden brown. Remove the roasted chickpeas from the tray, leaving the lining paper in place.

7 Mix the cashew nuts and turmeric together, spread out on the tray and roast for 5–7 minutes or until golden brown.

8 Add the dried apricots to the sauce and cook for a further 10 minutes.

9 Remove from the heat and stir through the herbs and roasted vegetables and chickpeas. Season to taste.

10 Sprinkle over the roasted cashew nuts and serve.

Portion out the vegetable tagine into appropriate containers (see pages 8–9). Leave to cool, then seal, label and date (see page 9) before freezing.

Microwave on high for 3 minutes, then remove from the microwave and stir. Re-cover but don't seal and microwave for a further 5 minutes or until piping hot. Leave to stand for 3 minutes before serving.

Preheat the oven to 160°C fan (350°F), Gas Mark 4. Uncover the ovenproof container and then cover the top with foil. Place on a baking sheet in the centre of the oven for 30–35 minutes or until piping hot. Leave to stand for 3 minutes before serving.

Wild mushroom risotto

You can use this risotto as a base recipe and add all kinds of seasonal vegetables: roasted butternut squash and tomatoes work well, or in the spring you can add crushed fresh peas, broad beans, lemon zest and mint.

Makes 6-7 portions **GF**

500g (1lb 2oz) chestnut mushrooms, quartered
olive oil
25g (1oz) dried wild mushrooms
400ml (14fl oz) water
salt and pepper

For the risotto base:
400ml (14fl oz) vegetable stock
125g (4½oz) unsalted butter
1 large onion, finely chopped
½ tablespoon finely chopped sage
3 thyme sprigs, leaves picked and finely chopped
400g (14oz) risotto rice, such as Arborio
150ml (5fl oz) white wine
100g (3½oz) Parmesan cheese, finely grated, plus extra shavings to garnish
handful of flat leaf parsley, leaves picked and chopped

1 Preheat the oven to 180°C fan (400°F), Gas Mark 6. Line a baking tray with nonstick baking paper. Spread the chestnut mushrooms out on the lined baking tray, season to taste and drizzle with olive oil. Roast for 10 minutes or until cooked through. Set aside.

2 Meanwhile, put the dried mushrooms in a pan, cover with the measured water and bring to the boil over a medium heat. Remove from the heat and leave the mushrooms to soak for 5–10 minutes or until rehydrated. Strain the liquid into a jug and reserve. Roughly chop the rehydrated mushrooms and set aside.

3 Pour the stock into a pan and bring to a gentle simmer. Melt 100g (3½oz) of the butter in a wide pan over a low heat. Add the onion and sweat for about 10 minutes until soft and translucent. Then add the sage and thyme and cook for a further 5 minutes.

4 Add the rice and stir until all the grains are well coated in the onion mixture. Then stir in the wine, turn up the heat and cook for 5 minutes until it has evaporated.

5 Gradually add the hot stock, a ladleful at a time, stirring after each addition until it is almost all absorbed, before adding the next. Continue until all the stock has been used up.

6 Add the mushroom soaking liquid and cook, stirring, until almost all absorbed and the rice is al dente – the whole process should take about 20–25 minutes. If you are freezing a batch, cook the rice for 2–3 minutes less.

7 Remove from the heat and beat in the grated Parmesan and the remaining butter until melted and incorporated. Then stir through all the mushrooms and parsley, season to taste and garnish with Parmesan shavings.

❄️ Portion out the risotto into appropriate containers (see pages 8–9), adding 2 tablespoons of water to each portion. Leave to cool, then seal, label and date (see page 9) before freezing.

Microwave on high for 3 minutes, then remove from the microwave and stir. Re-cover but don't seal and microwave for a further 5 minutes or until piping hot. Leave to stand for 3 minutes before serving.

Preheat the oven to 160°C fan (350°F), Gas Mark 4. Uncover the ovenproof container and then cover the top with foil. Place on a baking sheet in the centre of the oven for 30–35 minutes or until piping hot. Leave to stand for 3 minutes before serving.

Tomato & lentil soup

This healthy, comforting soup is perfect for a light lunch on the go or dinner. The lentils provide a valuable source of fibre and plant-based protein, among other nutritional benefits. Easy to make in a big batch, having a good stock of this soup in the freezer will do wonders for your midweek mealtimes.

Makes 8 portions **DF / GF / V / VE**

olive oil
1 large onion, roughly chopped
4 large carrots, roughly chopped
4 celery sticks, roughly chopped
2 garlic cloves, crushed
4 thyme sprigs, leaves picked and
    roughly chopped
1 teaspoon dried oregano
2 rosemary sprigs, leaves picked and
    roughly chopped
2 fresh bay leaves
2 × 400g (14oz) cans chopped tomatoes
800ml (1½ pints) vegetable stock
15g (½oz) basil, leaves picked and
    roughly chopped
300g (10½oz) cooked Puy lentils
salt and pepper

1 Heat a large, heavy-based pan over a medium heat. Add a good glug of olive oil and then the onion, carrots and celery with a pinch of salt and sweat about 10 minutes until the vegetables begin to soften.

2 Stir in the garlic, thyme, oregano, rosemary and bay leaves and cook for a further 5 minutes.

3 Pour in the chopped tomatoes and bring to a simmer, then reduce the heat and simmer gently for about 20 minutes, stirring occasionally.

4 Add the stock and cook for a further 20 minutes.

5 Remove from the heat, remove and discard the bay leaves, and then blitz with a hand blender or in a food processor or blender until smooth, adding more water if the consistency is too thick.

6 Stir through the basil and cooked lentils and season to taste. Heat through gently before serving.

Portion out the soup into appropriate containers (see pages 8–9). Leave to cool, then seal, label and date (see page 9) before freezing.

Microwave on high for 3 minutes, then remove from the microwave and stir. Re-cover but don't seal and microwave for a further 5 minutes or until piping hot. Leave to stand for 3 minutes before serving.

Put the container into a bowl of hot water and leave for a few minutes until the contents are loosened from the container sides. Transfer the contents to a pan and heat over a low heat until piping hot. Leave to stand for 3 minutes before serving.

Supergreens soup

You can vary the vegetables in this delicious soup depending on what you have to hand or what's in season. We have included whole mung beans, as they are rich in antioxidants and vitamins and also add a lovely texture to the soup. But any pulse would work, such as Puy lentils, or you can leave them out altogether.

Makes 8 portions **DF / GF / V / VE**

500g (1lb 2oz) dried whole mung beans, well rinsed and drained
olive oil
2 onions, finely chopped
4 celery sticks, finely chopped
3 garlic cloves, crushed
4 leeks, trimmed, cleaned and sliced
3 rosemary sprigs, leaves picked and roughly chopped
5 thyme sprigs, leaves picked and roughly chopped
1kg (2lb 4oz) courgettes, roughly chopped
1 vegetable stock cube
200g (7oz) spinach leaves
15g (½oz) flat leaf parsley, leaves picked and roughly chopped
15g (½oz) basil, leaves picked and roughly chopped, plus extra leaves to garnish
juice of ½ lemon
salt and pepper

1 Put the mung beans into a pan, cover with plenty of water and bring to the boil. Reduce the heat and simmer for about 30 minutes, stirring occasionally, until just cooked through, then drain.

2 While the beans are simmering, heat a large, heavy-based pan over a medium heat. Add a good glug of olive oil and then the onions and sweat for about 5–10 minutes until soft and translucent.

3 Add the celery and cook for 5 minutes. Then stir in the garlic, leeks, rosemary and thyme and cook for a further 5 minutes.

4 Add the courgettes and cook for about 10 minutes.

5 Crumble in the stock cube and cover the courgettes with water. Bring to the boil, then reduce the heat and simmer for about 15–20 minutes, stirring occasionally, until the courgettes are tender. Be careful not to overcook the soup, as this can cause the courgettes to taste bitter.

6 Remove the pan from the heat and stir in the spinach until it has wilted. Blitz with a hand blender or in a food processor or blender until smooth.

7 Stir through the herbs and lemon juice, and season to taste. Top with the cooked mung beans, and garnish with extra basil leaves. Heat through gently before serving.

❄ Portion out the soup and mung beans into appropriate containers (see pages 8–9). Leave to cool, then seal, label and date (see page 9) before freezing.

⊞ Microwave on high for 3 minutes, then remove from the microwave and stir. Re-cover but don't seal and microwave for a further 5 minutes or until piping hot. Leave to stand for 3 minutes before serving.

◎ Put the container into a bowl of hot water and leave for a few minutes until the contents are loosened from the container sides. Transfer the contents to a pan and heat over a low heat until piping hot. Leave to stand for 3 minutes before serving.

Thai sweet potato soup

The sweet potato makes this soup so luxuriously creamy and silky without the use of any dairy. It's perfect for a light lunch – take some into work with you to heat up quickly in the microwave. Healthy as well as delicious, a big batch of this in the freezer is a must!

Makes 6–8 portions **DF / GF / V / VE**

1 large onion, roughly chopped
3 lemon grass stalks, roughly chopped
2cm (¾-inch) piece of fresh root ginger, peeled and roughly chopped
4 garlic cloves, finely chopped
2 red chillies (or less, depending on how hot you like it), roughly chopped
1 teaspoon ground turmeric
2kg (4lb 8oz) sweet potatoes, peeled and roughly chopped
2 × 400ml (14fl oz) cans coconut milk
250ml (9fl oz) water
grated zest and juice of 1 lime
salt and pepper

To garnish (optional):
handful of fresh coriander leaves
red chilli slices

1 Put the onion, lemon grass, ginger, garlic and chilli into a food processor and blitz to a paste, adding a little water as necessary. Alternatively, use a hand blender.

2 Heat a large, heavy-based saucepan over a medium heat. Add the paste and turmeric and cook for about 5–10 minutes, stirring frequently.

3 Stir in the sweet potatoes and cook over a medium heat for 5 minutes.

4 Pour in the coconut milk and measured water, ensuring that the sweet potatoes are just covered with liquid, and bring to a simmer. Simmer for 10–15 minutes, stirring occasionally, until the potatoes are cooked through.

5 Remove from the heat and blitz with a hand blender or in a food processor or blender until smooth. Add the lime zest and juice and season to taste. Garnish with the coriander leaves and chilli slices, if using.

❄ Portion out the soup into appropriate containers (see pages 8–9). Leave to cool, then seal, label and date (see page 9) before freezing.

▣ Microwave on high for 3 minutes, then remove from the microwave and stir. Re-cover but don't seal and microwave for a further 5 minutes or until piping hot. Leave to stand for 3 minutes before serving.

◎ Put the container into a bowl of hot water and leave for a few minutes until the contents are loosened from the container sides. Transfer the contents to a pan and heat over a low heat until piping hot. Leave to stand for 3 minutes before serving.

Miso ramen

A savoury and comforting steaming bowl of broth, rice noodles and veg – perfect for a faff-free midweek dinner. If you are freezing this, don't cook the rice noodles too much to avoid overcooking them when reheating from frozen.

Makes 6–7 portions **DF / V / VE**

vegetable oil
200g (7oz) tofu, cut into slices 1cm
  (½ inch) thick
200g (7oz) chestnut mushrooms, sliced
50ml (2fl oz) teriyaki sauce
200g (7oz) butternut squash, peeled,
  deseeded and cut into slices 1cm
  (½ inch) thick
500g (1lb 2oz) dried rice noodles
200g (7oz) pak choi, sliced
salt and pepper

For the broth:
2 tablespoons coconut oil
1 onion, finely chopped
2 garlic cloves, crushed
2cm (¾-inch) piece of fresh root ginger,
  peeled and finely chopped
2 tablespoons medium curry powder
2 teaspoons ground coriander
2 teaspoons ground turmeric
50g (1¾oz) dark miso paste
2 teaspoons mirin
1 tablespoon nutritional yeast flakes
1 teaspoon Marmite
2 tablespoons dark soy sauce
1 teaspoon sugar
600ml (20fl oz) soya milk

1 For the broth, heat a large, heavy-based pan over a low heat. Add the coconut oil and the onion and sweat for 10 minutes until soft and translucent. Add the garlic and ginger and cook for 5 minutes. Then stir in the spices and cook for 2 minutes, stirring frequently.

2 Pour in 1 litre (1¾ pints) of water and then whisk in the miso paste, followed by the mirin, nutritional yeast flakes, Marmite, soy sauce and sugar. Bring to a simmer and cook for about 30 minutes, stirring occasionally, until reduced by half. Meanwhile, preheat the oven to 180°C fan (400°F), Gas Mark 6. Line a baking tray with nonstick baking paper.

3 Heat a glug of vegetable oil in a frying pan over a medium heat. Add the tofu in batches and cook until golden brown. Set aside in a bowl. Add the mushrooms to the pan and cook for 5 minutes, then transfer to the bowl. Pour over the teriyaki sauce and leave to marinate while you roast the squash.

4 Spread the squash slices out on the lined baking tray, drizzle with vegetable oil and season with salt and pepper. Roast for 15 minutes or until cooked through and slightly caramelized.

5 Add the soya milk to the broth and then blitz with a hand blender or in a food processor or blender until smooth. Season to taste with salt and return to a low heat.

6 Soak the noodles in boiling water for 3–5 minutes or until starting to soften, stirring occasionally, then drain and cool under cold running water.

7 Stir the pak choi into the broth until wilted, then remove from the heat.

8 To serve, portion out the noodles into bowls, then add the squash and mushrooms. Ladle over the broth and then top with the tofu.

Portion out the noodles, veg, broth and tofu into appropriate containers (see pages 8–9). Leave to cool, then seal, label and date (see page 9) before freezing.

Microwave on high for 3 minutes, then remove from the microwave and stir. Re-cover but don't seal and microwave for a further 5 minutes or until piping hot. Leave to stand for 3 minutes before serving.

Preheat the oven to 160°C fan (350°F), Gas Mark 4. Uncover the ovenproof container and then cover the top with foil. Place on a baking sheet in the centre of the oven for 40–45 minutes or until piping hot. Leave to stand for 3 minutes before serving.

Tofu or chicken fried rice

Makes 5-6 portions **DF** / **GF** / **V** and **VE** (if made with tofu)

500g (1lb 2oz) firm tofu, patted dry and cut into 4cm (1½-inch) cubes, or 4 boneless, skinless chicken thighs, cut into 4cm (1½-inch) chunks
2 tablespoons vegetable oil
2 garlic cloves, crushed
2cm (¾-inch) piece of fresh root ginger, peeled and finely chopped
2 red chillies, deseeded and finely chopped
3 red peppers, cored, deseeded and finely diced
400g (14oz) frozen peas
4 carrots, finely diced
500g (1lb 2oz) long-grain brown rice, cooked and drained (see page 133)
15g (½oz) fresh coriander, chopped
50g (1¾oz) spring onions, chopped
salt and pepper
1 tablespoon sesame seeds, to garnish (optional)

For the marinade:
2 tablespoons gluten-free dark soy sauce
5 tablespoons peanut butter
2 tablespoons harissa
3 tablespoons vegetable oil
1 tablespoon sesame oil
1 tablespoon maple syrup
2 garlic cloves, finely chopped

Who doesn't love fried rice? This recipe uses wholesome brown rice and is really filling, making the perfect meal for when you get back from work or the gym feeling really hungry and in need of something comforting yet healthy. You can use any kind of chicken meat, although thigh meat reheats better, or leftover cooked chicken.

1 Preheat the oven to 180°C fan (400°F), Gas Mark 6.

2 Put all the marinade ingredients into a food processor and blitz until smooth, or use a hand blender.

3 Place the tofu or chicken pieces in a bowl, add half the marinade and stir to coat, then season with salt. Spread out on a baking tray and bake for 25–30 minutes until the tofu is golden brown or the chicken is cooked through.

4 Heat a large frying pan over a medium heat. Add the vegetable oil and then the garlic, ginger and chillies and cook for 5 minutes.

5 Add the remaining marinade with the peppers, peas and carrots and cook for about 10 minutes until the vegetables start to soften.

6 Stir in the cooked rice and cook for a further 10 minutes.

7 Fold in the baked tofu along with the coriander and spring onions. If you are using chicken, shred the chicken meat before folding into the rice mixture.

8 Season to taste, then serve sprinkled with the sesame seeds.

Portion out the fried rice mixture into appropriate containers (see pages 8–9). Leave to cool, then seal, label and date (see page 9) before freezing.

Microwave on high for 3 minutes, then remove from the microwave and stir. Re-cover but don't seal and microwave for a further 5 minutes or until piping hot. Leave to stand for 3 minutes before serving.

Preheat the oven to 160°C fan (350°F), Gas Mark 4. Uncover the ovenproof container and then cover the top with foil. Place on a baking sheet in the centre of the oven for 35–40 minutes or until piping hot. Leave to stand for 3 minutes before serving.

Hearty
dinners

Famous chicken pie

This is Milly's favourite ByRuby dish. Crisp and flaky pastry on top of nourishing and hearty creamy chicken with bacon and sweet leeks, it's a real crowd-pleaser and ideal if you have people round for dinner at short notice.

Makes 8 pies

200g (7oz) unsalted butter
2 onions, finely chopped
4 leeks, trimmed, cleaned and
    finely chopped
2 garlic cloves, crushed
½ tablespoon chopped thyme leaves
500g (1lb 2oz) smoked streaky bacon,
    diced
30g (1oz) tarragon, leaves picked
    and chopped
30g (1oz) flat leaf parsley, leaves picked
    and chopped
2 tablespoons Dijon mustard
150g (5½oz) plain flour, plus extra for
    dusting if needed
1.5 litres (2⅔ pints) milk
1 medium chicken, about 1.5kg (3lb 5oz),
    roasted (see page 149), or leftover roast
    chicken, meat removed from the bone,
    skinned and shredded, about 500g
    (1lb 2oz) (reserve the carcass and/or
    bones for freezing and making stock –
    see page 149)
1 quantity of Fast & Flaky Pastry
    (see page 145) or 500g (1lb 2oz)
    puff pastry, in a block or ready-rolled
2 egg yolks, beaten
salt and pepper

1 Melt 50g (1¾oz) of the butter in a large pan over a medium heat, add the onions and leeks and sweat for about 10 minutes until soft and translucent.

2 Add the garlic and thyme and cook for 5 minutes. Then stir in the bacon and cook for 5 minutes.

3 Remove from the heat, add the herbs and 1 tablespoon of the mustard and season to taste. Leave to cool.

4 Melt the remaining butter in a saucepan over a low heat, stir in the flour until the mixture forms a roux (paste) and cook for about 5 minutes, stirring constantly. Then gradually add the milk, a little at a time, whisking constantly until it is all incorporated and the sauce is smooth and thick.

5 Remove from the heat, stir in the remaining mustard and season to taste. Leave to cool.

6 If eating now, preheat the oven to 180°C fan (400°F), Gas Mark 6.

7 Mix the roast chicken, white sauce and leek mixture together. Season to taste.

8 Divide the chicken mixture between individual pie or ovenproof dishes. Roll out the pastry on a lightly floured work surface, if not using ready-rolled, and cut out pieces large enough to cover the dishes. Trim and press to seal around the edges, then brush the pastry with the beaten egg yolks to glaze.

9 Place on a baking sheet and bake for 30–35 minutes or until the pastry is golden brown.

Portion out the chicken mixture into freezer-safe and ovenproof containers or dishes (see pages 8–9). Top with the pastry and glaze as above. Put the lids on or wrap tightly in clingfilm or foil, label and date (see page 9) before freezing.

Alternatively, use the recipe to make and freeze as one large pie, using a rectangular baking tin about 39.5 × 26cm (15½ × 10½ inches), 6.5cm (2½ inches) deep, but you will need to defrost it in the refrigerator overnight before baking for 45 minutes.

Preheat the oven to 160°C fan (350°F), Gas Mark 4. Uncover the ovenproof container or dish, place on a baking sheet and bake for 40–45 minutes or until the pastry is golden brown and the filling is piping hot.

Coconut chicken curry
with roasted cauliflower & chickpeas

Makes 10 portions **GF**

10 boneless, skinless chicken thighs
1 litre (1¾ pints) canned coconut milk
400g (14oz) can chopped tomatoes
2 large cauliflowers, florets and stalks
    cut into 2cm (¾-inch) chunks
400g (14oz) can chickpeas, drained
    and rinsed
1 teaspoon ground turmeric
vegetable oil
200g (7oz) baby spinach leaves
2 preserved lemons, drained, rinsed and
    rind finely chopped, pulp discarded
30g (1oz) fresh coriander, leaves picked
    and chopped
grated zest and juice of 2 limes
salt

For the marinade:
200g (7oz) natural yogurt
2cm (¾-inch) piece of fresh root ginger,
    peeled and roughly chopped
2½ tablespoons ground turmeric
2 tablespoons garam masala
1 tablespoon ground cumin
2 teaspoons chilli powder

For the curry paste:
2 tablespoons cumin seeds
2 tablespoons coriander seeds
2 tablespoons paprika
2 tablespoons garam masala
2 onions, roughly chopped
4 garlic cloves, roughly chopped
3cm (1¼-inch) piece of fresh root ginger,
    peeled and roughly chopped
50ml (2fl oz) sesame oil
30g (1oz) fresh coriander, roughly chopped
75g (2¾oz) desiccated coconut
5 red chillies, deseeded and
    roughly chopped

This aromatic, flavoursome curry has been a bestseller at ByRuby since day one. It holds completely true to our ethos of offering a healthy and simple alternative to a takeaway. It's great served with rice, Flatbreads (see page 146) or Naan Breads (see page 148) and some raita.

1 Put all the marinade ingredients into a food processor and blitz until smooth, adding a little water as necessary. Alternatively, use a hand blender.

2 Place the chicken in a bowl, add the marinade and stir to coat. Cover and leave to marinate in the refrigerator for at least 5 hours or overnight.

3 Put all the curry paste ingredients into a food processor and blitz until well combined but still chunky, or use a hand blender.

4 Heat a large, heavy-based pan over a medium heat. Add the curry paste with 2 teaspoons of salt and cook for 10 minutes, stirring frequently.

5 Add the chicken and marinade to the pan and cook for 10 minutes.

6 Stir in the coconut milk and tomatoes and simmer for around 30–35 minutes, stirring occasionally, until the chicken is cooked through and tender.

7 Meanwhile, preheat the oven to 180°C fan (400°F), Gas Mark 6.

8 Spread the cauliflower and chickpeas out on a baking tray, sprinkle with the turmeric, season with salt and drizzle with vegetable oil. Roast for 10 minutes or until the cauliflower is golden brown.

9 Add the roasted cauliflower and chickpeas to the curry sauce. Remove from the heat, then fold in the remaining ingredients, adjust the seasoning to taste and serve.

❄️ Portion out the chicken curry mixture into appropriate containers (see pages 8–9), with one chicken thigh per portion. Leave to cool, then seal, label and date (see page 9) before freezing.

Microwave on high for 3 minutes, then remove from the microwave and stir. Re-cover but don't seal and microwave for a further 5 minutes or until piping hot. Leave to stand for 3 minutes before serving.

Preheat the oven to 160°C fan (350°F), Gas Mark 4. Uncover the ovenproof container and then cover the top with foil. Place on a baking sheet in the centre of the oven for 40–45 minutes or until piping hot. Leave to stand for 3 minutes before serving.

Tarragon chicken

Always a huge success, this chicken dish is best served with our Fail-safe Mixed Rice with Parsley (see page 134) and some steamed mixed greens. That said, Milly loves stirring it through tagliatelle and serving it with a big crunchy green salad. Super versatile and super tasty, it's great for a cosy supper on your own but will equally make everyone happy at a dinner party with friends.

Makes 6 portions

12 boneless, skinless chicken thighs
1 teaspoon chopped thyme leaves
grated zest and juice of 2 lemons
50g (1¾oz) plain flour
vegetable oil
20g (¾oz) unsalted butter
2 onions, sliced
3 garlic cloves, crushed
350ml (12fl oz) white wine
1 chicken stock cube
400ml (14fl oz) double cream
30g (1oz) tarragon, chopped
1 tablespoon Dijon mustard
salt and pepper

To serve (optional):
Fail-safe Mixed Rice with Parsley
   (see page 134)
steamed mixed greens

1 Put the chicken thighs into a bowl, add the thyme, lemon zest and flour and toss to coat.

2 Heat a wide pan with a lid over a high heat and pour in enough vegetable oil to cover the base. Add the chicken thighs, in batches to avoid overcrowding the pan, and brown on both sides. Set aside on a plate.

3 Wipe out the pan with kitchen paper. Melt the butter in the pan over a low heat, add the onions and sweat for about 10 minutes until translucent.

4 Stir in the garlic and return the chicken to the pan. Cover with the wine and bring to a simmer, then reduce the heat and simmer gently for 5 minutes.

5 Crumble in the stock cube and pour in enough water to cover the chicken, then put a lid on the pan and simmer gently for 20 minutes, stirring occasionally, until the chicken is cooked through and tender.

6 Pour in the cream and cook for a further 5 minutes or until the sauce thickens.

7 Remove from the heat, then stir in the tarragon, lemon juice and mustard. Season to taste and serve with Fail-safe Mixed Rice with Parsley and steamed mixed greens, if you like.

Portion out the tarragon chicken mixture into appropriate containers (see pages 8–9), with 2 chicken thighs per portion. Leave to cool, then seal, label and date (see page 9) before freezing.

Microwave on high for 3 minutes, then remove from the microwave and stir. Re-cover but don't seal and microwave for a further 5 minutes or until piping hot. Leave to stand for 3 minutes before serving.

Preheat the oven to 160°C fan (350°F), Gas Mark 4. Uncover the ovenproof container and then cover the top with foil. Place on a baking sheet in the centre of the oven for 40–45 minutes or until piping hot. Leave to stand for 3 minutes before serving.

Sherry-braised chicken thighs

A true classic, my granny used to make this dish for dinner parties, and Delia Smith devised a similar recipe but featuring tarragon. The sage we use here gives it a lovely earthiness, and the extra crispy fried sage leaves are a nice finishing touch.

Makes 4 portions **GF**

8 bone-in, skin-on chicken thighs
vegetable oil
1 large onion, diced
4 garlic cloves, peeled but kept whole
2 tablespoons chopped sage, plus a
   few extra leaves to garnish
150ml (5fl oz) sherry vinegar
450ml (16fl oz) medium sherry
100ml (3½fl oz) double cream
salt and pepper

1 Season the chicken thighs all over with salt and pepper.

2 Heat a large, heavy-based pan with a lid over a high heat and add a good glug of vegetable oil. Then add the chicken thighs, in batches to avoid overcrowding the pan, and brown on both sides. Set aside on a plate.

3 Put a little more oil in the pan and then add the onion and garlic and sweat over a low heat for about 10 minutes until soft and translucent.

4 Add the chopped sage and cook, stirring, for about 30 seconds, then turn the heat up, pour in the sherry vinegar and sherry and bring to a simmer.

5 Return the chicken thighs to the pan along with any juices on the plate, placing them skin-side up, and simmer gently over a very low heat for about 40 minutes, stirring occasionally, until the chicken is cooked through and tender.

6 Remove the chicken from the sauce, then stir in the cream, turn the heat up and simmer for 2 minutes. Check and adjust the seasoning to taste.

7 Return the chicken to the pan. If eating now, heat a glug of vegetable oil in a frying pan over a high heat and fry a few extra sage leaves for about 30 seconds until crisp. Serve the chicken thighs sprinkled with the fried sage leaves.

❄️ Portion out the chicken mixture into appropriate containers (see pages 8–9), with 2 thighs per portion. Leave to cool, then seal, label and date (see page 9) before freezing.

〰️ Microwave on high for 3 minutes, then remove from the microwave and stir. Re-cover but don't seal and microwave for a further 5 minutes or until piping hot. Leave to stand for 3 minutes before serving, garnished with fried sage leaves as in the final step above.

🔲 Preheat the oven to 160°C fan (350°F), Gas Mark 4. Uncover the ovenproof container, then cover the top with foil. Place on a baking sheet in the centre of the oven for 25 minutes. Remove the foil and cook for 20 minutes, more, until piping hot. Leave to stand for 3 minutes before serving, garnished with fried sage leaves.

Smoky chicken
with chorizo & borlotti beans

My dad used to cook up this delicious piquant stew when we were young, and it brings back happy Spanish childhood memories for me. The addition of borlotti beans makes this dish a filling and fabulous one-pot meal.

Makes 8 portions **DF / GF** (if using gluten-free chorizo)

500g (1lb 2oz) dried borlotti beans
vegetable oil
1 large onion, finely chopped
4 carrots, finely chopped
4 celery sticks, finely chopped
4 garlic cloves, crushed
2 teaspoons cayenne pepper
½ tablespoon smoked paprika
1 tablespoon tomato purée
200ml (7fl oz) tomato ketchup
2 tablespoons Worcestershire sauce
½ tablespoon red wine vinegar
1 tablespoon caster sugar
500g (1lb 2oz) cooking chorizo sausage, cut into rounds 1cm (½ inch) thick
500g (1lb 2oz) canned chopped tomatoes
8 boneless, skinless chicken thighs
grated zest of 1 lemon
1 teaspoon chopped thyme leaves
600g (1lb 5oz) smoked streaky bacon
30g (1oz) flat leaf parsley, leaves picked and chopped
salt and pepper

1 Put the dried beans into a pan, cover with water and cook for an hour or until just soft but not mushy, then drain.

2 Meanwhile, heat a pan over a medium heat. Add a glug of vegetable oil and then the onion, carrots and celery and sweat for about 10 minutes until softened.

3 Add the garlic, cayenne pepper, smoked paprika and tomato purée and cook for 5 minutes.

4 Stir in the ketchup, Worcestershire sauce, vinegar, sugar and chorizo and cook for 5 minutes.

5 Pour in the tomatoes, reduce the heat and simmer gently for 10 minutes, stirring occasionally.

6 While you are preparing the sauce, preheat the oven to 180°C fan (400°F), Gas Mark 6.

7 Put the chicken thighs into a bowl, add the lemon zest and thyme and toss to coat.

8 Wrap each chicken thigh in 2 bacon slices, place on a baking tray and bake for 20–25 minutes or until cooked through.

9 Remove the sauce from the heat, stir through the cooked beans and parsley and season to taste.

10 To serve, divide the tomato and bean mixture between plates and place a chicken thigh on top.

Portion out the tomato and bean mixture into appropriate containers (see pages 8–9), then top each portion with a chicken thigh. Leave to cool, then seal, label and date (see page 9) before freezing.

Microwave on high for 3 minutes, then remove from the microwave and stir. Re-cover but don't seal and microwave for a further 5 minutes or until piping hot. Leave to stand for 3 minutes before serving.

Preheat the oven to 160°C fan (350°F), Gas Mark 4. Uncover the ovenproof container and then cover the top with foil. Place on a baking sheet in the centre of the oven for 40–45 minutes or until piping hot. Leave to stand for 3 minutes before serving.

Coq au vin

This is a classic dish that my grandmother often used to make. It's a classic for a reason – juicy chicken combined with salty bacon and earthy mushrooms in a rich red wine sauce – so it's a wonderful treat to have stored in the freezer to enjoy on an autumn evening with a baked potato or some mashed roots.

Makes 6 portions

6 skin-on chicken legs
50g (1¾oz) plain flour
vegetable oil
20g (¾oz) unsalted butter
1 onion, finely chopped
4 carrots, diced
3 celery sticks, diced
1 teaspoon chopped rosemary leaves
1 teaspoon chopped thyme leaves
2 garlic cloves, crushed
250g (9oz) smoked streaky bacon, diced
500g (1lb 2oz) chestnut mushrooms, quartered
1 tablespoon tomato purée
75cl bottle red wine
1 litre (1¾ pints) hot chicken stock
1 tablespoon Dijon mustard
15g (½oz) flat leaf parsley, leaves picked and chopped
salt and pepper

1 Put the chicken legs into a bowl, add the flour and toss to coat.

2 Heat a wide pan over a high heat and pour in enough vegetable oil to cover the base. Add the chicken legs, in batches to avoid overcrowding the pan, and brown them on both sides. Set aside on a plate.

3 Wipe out the pan with kitchen paper. Melt the butter in the pan over a low heat, add the onion with 2 teaspoons of salt and sweat for about 10 minutes until soft and translucent.

4 Add the carrots and celery and cook over a medium heat for 5 minutes. Then stir in the rosemary, thyme, garlic, bacon, mushrooms and tomato purée and cook for 5 minutes.

5 Return the chicken to the pan and pour over the wine. Simmer for about 10 minutes, stirring occasionally, until reduced.

6 Add the stock and enough water just to cover the chicken. Bring to a simmer, then reduce the heat and simmer gently for 25–30 minutes, stirring occasionally, until the chicken is cooked through and tender.

7 Remove from the heat, then stir in the mustard and parsley. Season to taste and serve.

Portion out the chicken mixture into appropriate containers (see pages 8–9), with one chicken leg per portion. Leave to cool, then seal, label and date (see page 9) before freezing.

Microwave on high for 3 minutes, then remove from the microwave and stir. Re-cover but don't seal and microwave for a further 5 minutes or until piping hot. Leave to stand for 3 minutes before serving.

Preheat the oven to 160°C fan (350°F), Gas Mark 4. Uncover the ovenproof container and then cover the top with foil. Place on a baking sheet in the centre of the oven for 40–45 minutes or until piping hot. Leave to stand for 3 minutes before serving.

Roasted salmon
with braised Puy lentils

This classic French recipe is such a warming and heartening dish, just what I crave on an autumnal day, and it's a complete meal in itself. The quality of the fish and its sustainability is really important, as with any fish dish. Trout also works very well here.

Makes 8-10 portions **GF**

500g (1lb 2oz) dried Puy lentils,
  well rinsed and drained
2 tablespoons vegetable oil
1 onion, finely chopped
3 large carrots, finely chopped
3 celery sticks, finely chopped
2 fresh bay leaves
5 thyme sprigs, leaves picked and
  finely chopped
2 garlic cloves, crushed
350ml (12fl oz) white wine
200ml (7fl oz) double cream
2 tablespoons Dijon mustard
200g (7oz) baby spinach leaves
30g (1oz) flat leaf parsley, leaves
  picked and chopped
grated zest and juice of 1 lemon
1 side of salmon, about 800g–1kg
  (1lb 12oz–2lb 4oz), skin and pin
  bones removed, cut into fillets
  about 100g (3½oz) each
salt and pepper

1 Put the lentils into a pan, cover with water and cook over a medium heat for 20 minutes or until just tender and not too mushy. Remove from the heat and drain.

2 Heat a pan over a low heat. Add the vegetable oil and then the onion and sweat for about 10 minutes until soft and translucent.

3 Add the carrots and celery and cook for about 5 minutes until starting to soften.

4 Stir in the bay leaves, thyme and garlic and cook for 10 minutes.

5 Pour in the wine and simmer for 5 minutes. Then stir in the cream and simmer for a further 5 minutes.

6 Meanwhile, if eating now, preheat the oven to 180°C fan (400°F), Gas Mark 6 for cooking the salmon with the lentils. If freezing, keep the salmon fillets raw.

7 Remove the lentil pan from the heat and remove and discard the bay leaves. Stir in the mustard, spinach, parsley and lemon zest and juice. Season to taste.

8 Transfer the lentil mixture to a baking dish and top with the salmon fillets. Season the salmon with salt and pepper and roast for 10–15 minutes or until the fish is just cooked through.

Portion out the lentil mixture into appropriate containers (see pages 8–9). Leave to cool, then top each portion with an uncooked salmon fillet. Seal, label and date (see page 9) before freezing.

Microwave on high for 3 minutes, then remove from the microwave and uncover. Re-cover but don't seal and microwave for a further 3 minutes or until piping hot. Leave to stand for 3 minutes before serving.

Preheat the oven to 160°C fan (350°F), Gas Mark 4. Uncover the ovenproof container and then cover the top with foil. Place on a baking sheet in the centre of the oven for 30–35 minutes or until piping hot. Leave to stand for 3 minutes before serving.

Ruby's fabulous fish pie

This meal has been number one of the top sellers at ByRuby since the beginning and there is a reason for that. It's so moreish, comforting and delicious! You can use any fish you fancy here, but as we always say, make sure it's sustainable.

Makes 10–12 portions

1 side of smoked haddock, about 600g (1lb 5oz), skin and pin bones removed
1 side of coley or any white fish, about 600g (1lb 5oz), skin and pin bones removed
1 side of salmon, about 600g (1lb 5oz), skin and pin bones removed
3kg (6lb 8oz) potatoes, peeled and quartered
2 tablespoons vegetable oil
1 large onion, finely chopped
5 leeks, trimmed, cleaned and finely chopped
15g (½oz) thyme, leaves picked and finely chopped
3 garlic cloves, crushed
50g (1¾oz) unsalted butter
2 teaspoons salt
1 teaspoon freshly grated nutmeg
1 teaspoon pepper
30g (1oz) flat leaf parsley, leaves picked and finely chopped
grated zest and juice of 1 lemon
4 tablespoons grated Cheddar cheese (optional)
salt and pepper

For the white sauce:
150g (5½oz) unsalted butter
150g (5½oz) plain flour
1.5 litres (2⅔ pints) milk

1 Preheat the oven to 180°C fan (400°F), Gas Mark 6.

2 Put the haddock into a pan, cover with water and bring to the boil over a medium heat, then drain and set aside.

3 Place the coley and salmon on a baking tray and bake for about 10–12 minutes or until the fish is just cooked through. Set aside but leave the oven on if eating now.

4 Cook the potatoes in a large pan of salted boiling water for about 15 minutes until cooked through.

5 Meanwhile, heat a pan over a low heat. Add the vegetable oil and then the onion and leeks and sweat for about 10 minutes until soft and translucent.

6 Add the thyme and garlic and cook for a further 5 minutes.

7 Drain the potatoes, return to the pan and add the butter, salt, nutmeg and pepper. Mash the potatoes with a potato masher or a fork – I like my mash slightly chunky but you can go ultra smooth if you prefer.

8 For the sauce, melt the butter in a saucepan over a low heat, stir in the flour until it forms a roux and cook for about 5 minutes, stirring constantly. Then gradually add the milk, a little at a time, whisking constantly until it is all incorporated and the sauce is smooth and thick. Remove from the heat and season to taste.

9 Mix the cooked fish, white sauce and onion and leek mixture together gently, ensuring that the fish remains in large chunks for added texture. Then fold in the parsley and lemon zest and juice and season to taste.

10 If eating now, transfer the fish mixture to a baking dish, top with the mashed potatoes and sprinkle with the grated Cheddar, if using. Bake for 30–35 minutes or until the top is golden and the filling is piping hot.

❄ Portion out the fish pie filling into freezer-safe and ovenproof containers or dishes (see pages 8–9), then top with the mashed potatoes and add a sprinkle of grated Cheddar, if using. Leave to cool. Put the lids on or wrap tightly in clingfilm or foil, label and date (see page 9) before freezing.

▦ Preheat the oven to 160°C fan (350°F), Gas Mark 4. Uncover the ovenproof container, place on a baking sheet and bake for 40–45 minutes, until the top is golden and the filling is piping hot.

Sri Lankan hake

This recipe brings back happy memories and tastes from a trip to Sri Lanka. The spice mix recipe makes plenty for storing in a jar for up to six months and using as the base for other curries or as a marinade for roasted vegetables, fish or meat.

Makes 6–8 portions **DF / GF**

vegetable oil
1 large onion, diced
2 garlic cloves, crushed
2 red chillies, deseeded and chopped
4 fresh curry leaves
1 teaspoon black mustard seeds
3 tablespoons Curry Powder (see below)
400g (14oz) can chopped tomatoes
400ml (14fl oz) can coconut milk
400g (14oz) can chickpeas, drained
    and rinsed
2 teaspoons ground turmeric
200g (7oz) baby spinach leaves
15g (½oz) fresh coriander, leaves chopped
juice of ½ lime
1 × 800g (1lb 12oz) side of hake, skin and pin
    bones removed, cut into 100g (3½oz) fillets
salt and pepper

For the curry powder:
2 teaspoons coriander seeds
1 teaspoon cumin seeds
1 star anise
1 small cinnamon stick
1 teaspoon fennel seeds
½ teaspoon pepper
½ teaspoon fenugreek seeds
½ teaspoon chilli flakes

1 Put all the curry powder ingredients into a spice grinder and grind to a powder, or use a pestle and mortar.

2 Heat a large, heavy-based pan over a medium heat. Add a glug of vegetable oil and then the onion and sweat for about 10 minutes until soft and translucent.

3 Add the crushed garlic, chillies, curry leaves, mustard seeds and 2 tablespoons of the curry powder and cook for about 5 minutes until aromatic, stirring frequently.

4 Pour in the tomatoes and coconut milk and bring to a simmer. Then reduce the heat and simmer gently for 20–30 minutes, stirring occasionally, until the sauce has thickened.

5 Meanwhile, if eating now, preheat the oven to 180°C fan (400°F), Gas Mark 6.

6 Toss the chickpeas in the turmeric, spread out on a baking tray and roast for 10 minutes or until golden brown. Set aside. If eating now, leave the oven on for cooking the hake fillets with the curry sauce. If freezing, keep the hake fillets raw and turn the oven off.

7 Remove the curry sauce from the heat and stir through the roasted chickpeas, spinach, coriander and lime juice. Season to taste.

8 If eating now, transfer the curry sauce to a baking dish, top with the hake fillets and sprinkle with the remaining 1 tablespoon of curry powder along with a little salt. Bake for 10–15 minutes or until the fish is just cooked through.

❄️ Portion out the curry sauce mixture into suitable containers (see pages 8–9). Leave to cool, then top each portion with an uncooked hake fillet and add a little sprinkle of the curry powder and salt. Seal, label and date (see page 9) before freezing.

🔲 Microwave on high for 3 minutes, then remove from the microwave, uncover and agitate the container gently from side to side. Re-cover but don't seal and microwave for a further 3 minutes or until piping hot. Leave to stand for 3 minutes before serving.

🔲 Preheat the oven to 160°C fan (350°F), Gas Mark 4. Uncover the ovenproof container and then cover the top with foil. Place on a baking sheet in the centre of the oven for 30–35 minutes or until piping hot. Leave to stand for 3 minutes before serving.

Fragrant trout
with pak choi

This recipe is not only packed full of flavour but is also very nourishing and healthy, plus it's easy to prepare and great reheated from frozen to make mealtimes a breeze. Enjoy as a lovely light dish on its own, or serve with rice noodles or our Fail-safe Mixed Rice with Parsley (see page 134).

Makes 8-10 portions **DF / GF**

1 side of trout, about 800g–1kg
(1lb 12oz–2lb 4oz), skin and pin bones removed, cut into fillets about 100g (3½oz) each
2½ tablespoons Thai red curry paste
2 tablespoons sesame oil
3 fresh kaffir lime leaves
1 tablespoon fish sauce
2 × 400ml (14fl oz) cans coconut milk
30g (1oz) fresh coriander, leaves picked and finely chopped, plus extra leaves (optional) to garnish
grated zest and juice of 1 lime
500g (1lb 2oz) pak choi, roughly chopped
1 tablespoon gluten-free dark soy sauce
200g (7oz) frozen or fresh edamame beans

For the marinade:
2 red chillies, deseeded and finely chopped
2cm (¾-inch) piece of fresh root ginger, peeled and finely chopped
2 tablespoons clear honey
grated zest of 1 lime
2 tablespoons gluten-free dark soy sauce

1 Place the trout fillets in a bowl, add all the marinade ingredients and rub them all over the fish. Cover and leave to marinate in the refrigerator while you prepare the sauce.

2 Heat a large, heavy-based pan over a low heat. Add the curry paste with the sesame oil and cook for 5 minutes or until aromatic, stirring frequently.

3 Stir in the lime leaves, fish sauce and coconut milk and simmer gently for about 20–25 minutes, stirring occasionally, until the sauce starts to thicken.

4 Meanwhile, if eating now, preheat the oven to 180°C fan (400°F), Gas Mark 6 for cooking the trout with the sauce. If freezing, keep the trout fillets raw.

5 Remove the sauce from the heat and stir in the chopped coriander, lime zest and juice, pak choi, soy sauce and edamame.

6 If eating now, transfer the sauce to a baking dish and top with the trout fillets. Roast for 10–15 minutes or until the fish is just cooked through. Serve garnished with a few extra coriander leaves, if you like.

Portion out the sauce into appropriate containers (see pages 8–9). Leave to cool, then top each portion with a marinated uncooked trout fillet. Seal, label and date (see page 9) before freezing.

Microwave on high for 3 minutes, then remove from the microwave, uncover and agitate the container gently from side to side. Re-cover but don't seal and microwave for a further 3 minutes or until piping hot. Leave to stand for 3 minutes before serving.

Preheat the oven to 160°C fan (350°F), Gas Mark 4. Uncover the ovenproof container and then cover the top with foil. Place on a baking sheet in the centre of the oven for 30–35 minutes or until piping hot. Leave to stand for 3 minutes before serving.

Roasted white fish
with cannellini beans, slow-roasted tomatoes & leeks

This flavourful recipe is ideal for a summer evening or a working lunch. Slow-roasting the tomatoes helps to bring out their sugars, so even if you're making this in winter you can still get a great tomato flavour that will transport you back to summertime. A squeeze of lemon juice to serve adds the perfect finishing touch.

Makes 6–8 portions **DF / GF**

1 side of white fish, such as hake or cod, about 600–800g (1lb 5oz–1lb 12oz), skin and pin bones removed, cut into fillets about 100g (3½oz) each
500g (1lb 2oz) dried white beans, such as cannellini or haricot
250g (9oz) cherry tomatoes, halved
1 teaspoon sugar
6 thyme sprigs, leaves picked and finely chopped
vegetable oil
1 onion, finely chopped
3 celery sticks, finely chopped
2 leeks, trimmed, cleaned and finely chopped
2 garlic cloves, finely chopped
2 teaspoons fennel seeds
2 rosemary sprigs, leaves picked and finely chopped
350ml (12fl oz) white wine
1 litre (1¾ pints) hot chicken stock
30g (1oz) flat leaf parsley, leaves picked and chopped
juice of 1 lemon
salt and pepper

For the marinade:
30g (1oz) flat leaf parsley, leaves picked and finely chopped
10g (¼oz) thyme, leaves picked and finely chopped
grated zest of 1 lemon
2 tablespoons olive oil
2 garlic cloves, crushed
2 teaspoons fennel seeds, crushed

1 Preheat the oven to 150°C fan (335°F), Gas Mark 3½.

2 Place the white fish fillets in a bowl, add all the marinade ingredients and rub them all over the fish. Cover and leave to marinate in the refrigerator while you prepare the rest of the dish.

3 Put the beans into a pan, cover with water and bring to the boil. Boil rapidly for 10 minutes, then reduce the heat and simmer for about 45 minutes–1½ hours, stirring occasionally, until soft but not mushy, depending on the type of bean. Drain and set aside.

4 Meanwhile, arrange the halved tomatoes, cut-side up, on a baking tray and sprinkle over the sugar, chopped thyme leaves and 1 teaspoon of salt. Roast for 25–30 minutes, ensuring that they don't colour too much. Set aside.

5 If eating now, turn the oven up to 180°C fan (400°F), Gas Mark 6 for cooking the fish fillets with the beans. If freezing, keep the marinated fish fillets raw and turn the oven off.

6 Heat a little vegetable oil in a pan over a medium heat. Add the onion and sweat for about 10 minutes until soft and translucent.

7 Add the celery and leeks and cook for 5 minutes. Then add the garlic, fennel seeds and rosemary and cook for a further 3 minutes.

8 Stir in the cooked beans and wine and cook for 5 minutes, then pour in the stock and simmer for 10 minutes, stirring occasionally.

9 Remove from the heat, add the parsley and lemon juice and season to taste.

10 If eating now, transfer the bean mixture to a baking dish, top with the fish fillets and roast for 10–15 minutes or until the fish is just cooked through. Serve with the roasted tomatoes on top.

❄ Portion out the bean mixture into appropriate containers (see pages 8–9). Leave to cool, then top each portion with a marinated uncooked fish fillet and scatter over the cooled roasted tomatoes. Seal, label and date (see page 9) before freezing.

〰 Microwave on high for 3 minutes, then remove from the microwave, uncover and agitate the container gently from side to side. Re-cover but don't seal and microwave for a further 3 minutes or until piping hot. Leave to stand for 3 minutes before serving.

▦ Preheat the oven to 160°C fan (350°F), Gas Mark 4. Uncover the ovenproof container and then cover the top with foil. Place on a baking sheet in the centre of the oven for 30–35 minutes or until piping hot. Leave to stand for 3 minutes before serving.

Sausages
with lentils & chorizo

This dish is wonderfully nourishing and cheering for a chilly night, and using the best sausages, pancetta and chorizo you can afford will really make a difference to the flavour. Serve with some lovely crusty bread and a crisp green salad dressed with our Classic Vinaigrette (see page 145), or some sautéed Swiss chard.

Makes 4 portions

olive oil
1 large onion, diced
2 garlic cloves, sliced
8 large sausages
200g (7oz) cooking chorizo sausage, skinned and cut into 5mm (¼-inch) cubes
100g (3½oz) pancetta or bacon, diced
1 teaspoon smoked paprika
200g (7oz) dried Puy lentils, well rinsed and drained
400g (14oz) can chopped tomatoes or 500g (1lb 2oz) passata
250ml (9fl oz) red wine
500–600ml (18–20fl oz) water
1–2 fresh bay leaves
salt and pepper
wilted Swiss chard, to serve (optional)

1 Preheat the oven to 200°C fan (425°F), Gas Mark 7.

2 Meanwhile, heat a large, heavy-based pan with a lid over a low heat. Add a good glug of olive oil and then the onion and garlic with a pinch of salt and sweat for about 5 minutes or until the onion is translucent.

3 Lay the sausages on a baking tray and pierce each one a couple of times with a fork. Bake for 20–30 minutes or until browned.

4 Meanwhile, add the chorizo and pancetta or bacon to the onion and garlic, turn the heat up and cook until the meat starts to brown, stirring constantly, then add the smoked paprika.

5 Stir the lentils into the pan, pour in the tomatoes or passata, wine and 500ml (18fl oz) of the measured water and add the bay leaf or leaves and some salt and pepper. Bring to a simmer.

6 Put the lid on the pan, reduce the heat and simmer gently for about 10 minutes, stirring occasionally.

7 Add the browned sausages, replace the lid and continue to simmer gently for a further 10 minutes or until the lentils are cooked through, adding the remaining water as necessary to avoid the mixture becoming too dry. Remove and discard the bay leaf or leaves.

8 If eating now, season to taste and serve with sautéed Swiss chard, if you like.

Portion out the lentil mixture into appropriate containers (see pages 8–9), with 2 sausages per portion. Leave to cool, then seal, label and date (see page 9) before freezing.

Microwave on high for 3 minutes, then remove from the microwave and stir. Re-cover but don't seal and microwave for a further 5 minutes or until piping hot. Leave to stand for 3 minutes before serving.

Preheat the oven to 160°C fan (350°F), Gas Mark 4. Uncover the ovenproof container and then cover the top with foil. Place on a baking sheet in the centre of the oven for 40–45 minutes or until piping hot. Leave to stand for 3 minutes before serving.

Milly's wedding lamb tagine

I got married in Lancashire, North West England, in the month of March, where this tagine fed the hungry wedding party and warmed the cockles as the vaguely spring-like afternoon turned into a chilly wintry evening. Warmingly spiced and slightly sweet with apricots, this dish will please any crowd.

Makes 6–8 portions **GF**

1kg (2lb 4oz) boneless lamb leg or
   shoulder, diced
vegetable oil
3 onions, finely diced
4 garlic cloves, sliced
grated zest of 1 lemon
1 tablespoon sweet paprika
2 teaspoons ground cinnamon
2 teaspoons ground cumin
2 teaspoons ground coriander
2 teaspoons ground turmeric
1 teaspoon hot paprika
2 red peppers, cored, deseeded and sliced
400g (14oz) dried apricots, chopped
2 × 400g (14oz) cans chopped tomatoes
750ml (1⅓ pints) hot beef or lamb stock
400g (14oz) can chickpeas, drained
   and rinsed
handful each of mint and fresh coriander
   leaves, roughly chopped
salt and pepper
natural yogurt, to serve

1 Preheat the oven to 160°C fan (350°F), Gas Mark 4.

2 Season the lamb all over with salt and pepper.

3 Heat a large, heavy-based ovenproof pan with a lid over a high heat and add a good glug of vegetable oil. Then add the lamb, in batches to avoid overcrowding the pan, and brown all over. Set aside on a plate.

4 Add another glug of oil to the pan and then the onions and garlic with the lemon zest and a pinch of salt and sweat over a low heat for about 10 minutes until soft and translucent.

5 Add all the spices and cook, stirring, until fragrant. Then stir in the red peppers and apricots, turn up the heat and stir-fry for about a minute.

6 Return the lamb to the pan with any meat juices on the plate and pour in the tomatoes and stock. Bring to a simmer, cover the pan with the lid and transfer to the oven. Cook for about 2 hours or until the lamb is falling apart, stirring halfway through.

7 Remove from the oven, stir in the chickpeas and herbs and leave to stand for 15 minutes. Season to taste and serve with a dollop of natural yogurt on each plate.

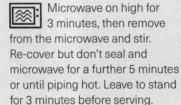 Portion out the tagine mixture into appropriate containers (see pages 8–9). Leave to cool, then seal, label and date (see page 9) before freezing.

Microwave on high for 3 minutes, then remove from the microwave and stir. Re-cover but don't seal and microwave for a further 5 minutes or until piping hot. Leave to stand for 3 minutes before serving.

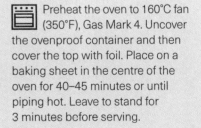 Preheat the oven to 160°C fan (350°F), Gas Mark 4. Uncover the ovenproof container and then cover the top with foil. Place on a baking sheet in the centre of the oven for 40–45 minutes or until piping hot. Leave to stand for 3 minutes before serving.

Slow-cooked lamb
with caponata & salsa verde

This extra-special dish is perfect for a celebratory event. Our friend and *Masterchef* finalist, Claire Fyfe, masterminded this recipe and we worked on it together to make it freezer friendly. Making it ahead and then reheating it on the day will give you more time to spend with family and friends rather than slaving away in the kitchen. Serve with some jumbo couscous and herbs.

Makes 10–12 portions **DF / GF**

2kg (4lb 8oz) bone-in lamb shoulder
8 thyme sprigs
3 fresh bay leaves
8 garlic cloves, sliced
8 salted anchovy fillets, halved lengthways
6 rosemary sprigs, leaves picked
75cl bottle white wine
1 litre (1¾ pints) water
1 quantity of Salsa Verde (see page 141)

For the caponata:
5 aubergines, cut into 2cm (¾-inch) chunks
vegetable oil
4 red onions, diced
4 garlic cloves, sliced
2 × 400g (14oz) cans chopped tomatoes
1 tablespoon capers
2 teaspoons dried oregano
50ml (2fl oz) red wine vinegar
15g (½oz) flat leaf parsley, leaves picked
  and roughly chopped
salt and pepper

1 Preheat the oven to 180°C fan (400°F), Gas Mark 6.

2 Put the lamb shoulder into a large baking dish and then dot around the thyme sprigs and bay leaves. Using a small sharp knife, carefully cut 16 small slits at regular intervals into the top surface of the lamb, then push the garlic slices, anchovies and rosemary leaves into each slit. Pour over the wine and measured water.

3 Cover the dish with nonstick baking paper and then foil to make sure no moisture can escape. Cook for about 2–3 hours, depending on the size of the joint, or until the meat is falling off the bone.

4 Meanwhile, for the caponata, spread the aubergine chunks out on a baking tray, drizzle with vegetable oil and roast for 20 minutes or until golden brown and cooked through.

5 While the aubergine is roasting, heat a pan over a low heat. Add a glug of vegetable oil and then the onions and garlic and sweat for about 10 minutes until soft and translucent.

6 Add the tomatoes, capers and oregano and simmer gently for about 30–35 minutes, stirring occasionally, until the sauce has thickened. Add the vinegar and parsley and season to taste, then stir through the roasted aubergine.

7 Remove the lamb from the oven and leave until cool enough to touch, then shred the meat from the bone and pour over the juices.

8 To serve, spoon the caponata on to plates and pile the lamb on top, followed by a large spoonful of the salsa verde.

❄ Portion out the caponata into appropriate containers (see pages 8–9), then top with an equal quantity of the lamb and add a large spoonful of the salsa verde. Leave to cool, then seal, label and date (see page 9) before freezing.

🔲 Microwave on high for 3 minutes, then remove from the microwave and stir. Re-cover but don't seal and microwave for a further 5 minutes or until piping hot. Leave to stand for 3 minutes before serving.

🔲 Preheat the oven to 160°C fan (350°F), Gas Mark 4. Uncover the ovenproof container and then cover the top with foil. Place on a baking sheet in the centre of the oven for 40–45 minutes or until piping hot. Leave to stand for 3 minutes before serving.

Slowly braised beef ragu
with pappardelle pasta

This is a recipe my stepmother gave to me – she's half Italian and knows her stuff. The sauce is seriously rich and moreish, although it takes a while to cook in the oven, but it's so worth it. Having a batch of this in the freezer is pure joy when you need a midweek pick-me-up.

I love serving any pasta dish with a crunchy green salad. Fresh and firm Little Gem leaves work brilliantly torn apart and combined with fragrant herby leaves, like rocket or pea shoots, perhaps a handful of chopped coriander, parsley or chives. The supermarkets often sell a ready-made bag of mixed herby leaves, which can make your life easier. Radishes chopped into quarters add a wonderful peppery piquancy, or raw carrot ribbons, shaved with a potato peeler, are great for extra crunch. Our Classic Vinaigrette (see page 145) will pep up any salad leaves beautifully.

Makes 8–10 portions

1kg (2lb 4oz) dried pappardelle pasta
finely grated Parmesan cheese, to serve (optional)

For the ragu:
1kg (2lb 4oz) beef brisket, cut into 2cm (¾-inch) chunks
1 large onion, finely diced
4 large carrots, finely diced
4 celery sticks, finely diced
4 garlic cloves, crushed
4 rosemary sprigs, leaves picked and roughly chopped
6 thyme sprigs, leaves picked and roughly chopped
1 teaspoon chopped sage leaves
2 fresh bay leaves
1 tablespoon tomato purée
75cl bottle red wine
400g (14oz) can chopped tomatoes
500ml (18fl oz) hot beef stock
2 teaspoons salt

1 Preheat the oven to 180°C fan (400°F), Gas Mark 6.

2 Put all the ragu ingredients into a deep roasting tray and mix together, making sure there is enough liquid to cover the beef and topping up with water if necessary. Cover with nonstick baking paper so that it sits directly on top of the beef mixture, then cover the tray tightly with foil to make sure no moisture can escape.

3 Cook for 3–4 hours or until the beef is falling apart, then remove and discard the bay leaves.

4 Meanwhile, make the tomato sauce. Heat a large pan over a medium heat. Add 2 tablespoons of vegetable oil and then the onion and sweat for about 10 minutes until soft and translucent.

5 Add the carrots and celery and cook for about 5 minutes until the vegetables start to soften. Then add the garlic, rosemary, thyme, oregano and tomato purée and cook for a further 5 minutes.

6 Stir in the tomatoes, sugar and 1 teaspoon of salt, reduce the heat and simmer gently for 40–45 minutes, stirring occasionally, until the sauce has thickened. Remove from the heat, add the basil and parsley and season to taste.

7 Once the beef is ready, shred the meat with a fork, then stir the ragu into the tomato sauce.

8 Cook the pasta in a large pan of salted boiling water according to the packet instructions, for about 8 minutes, until al dente.

Continued overleaf ...

For the tomato sauce:
vegetable oil
1 large onion, finely chopped
4 large carrots, diced
4 large celery sticks, finely chopped
3 garlic cloves, crushed
3 rosemary sprigs, leaves picked and
    finely chopped
4 thyme sprigs, leaves picked and
    finely chopped
2 teaspoons dried oregano
1 tablespoon tomato purée
2 × 400g (14oz) cans chopped tomatoes
2 teaspoons sugar
30g (1oz) basil, leaves picked and
    finely chopped
30g (1oz) flat leaf parsley, leaves picked
    and finely chopped
salt and pepper

For the gremolata (optional):
15g (½oz) flat leaf parsley, leaves picked
    and finely chopped
grated zest of 2 lemons
1 garlic clove, crushed

9 While the pasta is cooking, mix the gremolata ingredients together in a bowl, if using.

10 To serve, drain the pasta and mix 3 tablespoons of the ragu sauce through the hot pasta. Divide the pasta between plates, followed by the remaining ragu sauce. Then sprinkle over the gremolata, if using, and a good grating of Parmesan, if you like.

 Portion out the ragu-dressed pasta into appropriate containers (see pages 8–9), then top with an equal quantity of the remaining ragu sauce and a sprinkle of the gremolata, if using. Leave to cool, then seal, label and date (see page 9) before freezing.

 Microwave on high for 3 minutes, then remove from the microwave and stir. Re-cover but don't seal and microwave for a further 5 minutes or until piping hot. Leave to stand for 3 minutes before serving with a good grating of Parmesan, if you like.

Preheat the oven to 160°C fan (350°F), Gas Mark 4. Uncover the ovenproof container and then cover the top with foil. Place on a baking sheet in the centre of the oven for 40–45 minutes or until piping hot. Leave to stand for 3 minutes before serving with a grating of Parmesan, if you like.

Classic beef bourguignon

This is always a hit for a dinner party or a cosy solo supper at home alone. Choosing good-quality beef – chuck steak is an ideal cut to use – and cooking it low and slow ensures a full-flavoured and meltingly tender result. This dish tastes far better if it's left for a day after cooking so that the flavours have time to intensify and penetrate the meat. Serve with a baked potato or tagliatelle... yum, yum, yum!

Makes 8 portions **DF**

1.5kg (3lb 5oz) stewing beef, such as chuck, cut into 2cm (¾-inch) chunks
50g (1¾oz) plain flour
vegetable oil
2 large onions, diced
10 large carrots, 5 diced, 5 cut into large chunks
4 celery sticks, diced
5 thyme sprigs, leaves picked and finely chopped
3 rosemary sprigs, leaves picked and finely chopped
3 garlic cloves, crushed
2 fresh bay leaves
1 tablespoon tomato purée
200g (7oz) smoked streaky bacon, diced
75cl bottle red wine
1 litre (1¾ pints) hot beef stock
500ml (18fl oz) water
500g (1lb 2oz) chestnut mushrooms, quartered
2 tablespoons Dijon mustard
15g (½oz) flat leaf parsley, leaves picked and chopped
salt and pepper

1 Put the beef chunks into a bowl, add the flour and toss to coat.

2 Heat a large, heavy-based pan over a high heat and pour in enough vegetable oil to cover the base. Add the beef, in batches to avoid overcrowding the pan, and brown all over. Set aside on a plate.

3 Wipe out the pan with kitchen paper. Add 1 tablespoon of oil and then the onions with 1 teaspoon of salt and sweat over a low heat for about 10 minutes until soft and translucent.

4 Add the diced carrots and celery and cook for about 10 minutes until the vegetables are softened.

5 Stir in the thyme, rosemary, garlic, bay leaves and tomato purée and cook for 5 minutes. Then add the bacon and cook for a further 5 minutes.

6 Return the beef to the pan and pour over the wine. Reduce the heat and simmer gently for 15 minutes, stirring occasionally.

7 Pour in the stock and measured water and bring to the boil, then reduce the heat and simmer gently for 35 minutes, stirring occasionally.

8 Stir in the mushrooms and carrot chunks and simmer gently for a further hour or so until the beef is falling apart, stirring occasionally and adding water as necessary to avoid the sauce becoming too dry.

9 Remove from the heat and remove and discard the bay leaves. Stir in the mustard and parsley. Season to taste and serve.

Portion out the beef mixture into appropriate containers (see pages 8–9). Leave to cool, then seal, label and date (see page 9) before freezing.

Microwave on high for 3 minutes, then remove from the microwave and stir. Re-cover but don't seal and microwave for a further 5 minutes or until piping hot. Leave to stand for 3 minutes before serving.

Preheat the oven to 160°C fan (350°F), Gas Mark 4. Uncover the ovenproof container and then cover the top with foil. Place on a baking sheet in the centre of the oven for 40–45 minutes or until piping hot. Leave to stand for 3 minutes before serving.

Thai beef curry

This knockout dish is inspired by those I enjoyed on the streets of Southern Thailand. It's a beautifully balanced one-pot dish that is easy to make and great to have ready to go in the freezer. Serve with some jasmine rice or sticky rice.

Makes 8–10 portions **DF / GF**

vegetable oil
1 onion, roughly chopped
2kg (4lb 8oz) stewing beef, such as chuck, cut into 2cm (¾-inch) chunks
3 × 400ml (14fl oz) cans coconut milk
1 beef stock cube
6 fresh kaffir lime leaves, thinly sliced
seeds from 4 cardamom pods
30g (1oz) Thai basil, leaves picked and stalks reserved, both roughly chopped
4 heads of pak choi, roughly chopped
50g (1¾oz) cashew nuts, toasted and roughly chopped
juice of 1 lime, or more to taste
30g (1oz) fresh coriander, roughly chopped (optional)
salt and pepper

For the curry paste:
2 tablespoons coriander seeds
2 tablespoons cumin seeds
3 red chillies, deseeded for a milder flavour
3 tablespoons Thai red curry paste
3 tablespoons fish sauce, plus extra (optional) to taste
1 teaspoon chilli powder (optional)
3 lemon grass stalks, roughly chopped
grated zest of 2 limes

1 Heat a large, heavy-based pan over a medium heat. Add a good glug of vegetable oil and then the onion and sweat for about 10 minutes until softened.

2 Meanwhile, put all the curry paste ingredients into a food processor and blitz to a paste, adding a little water as necessary. Alternatively, use a hand blender.

3 Add the curry paste to the pan and cook for about 2–3 minutes until aromatic, stirring frequently. Then stir in the beef and cook for about 10 minutes.

4 Pour in the coconut milk, crumble in the stock cube and add the lime leaves, cardamom seeds and chopped Thai basil stalks. Cover the pan and simmer gently for about 2–3 hours, stirring occasionally, until the beef is falling apart.

5 Stir in the pak choi, cashew nuts, lime juice and the chopped Thai basil leaves, along with the coriander, if using. Season to taste and add more lime juice or fish sauce to taste, if you like.

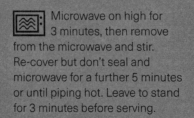 Portion out the curry mixture into appropriate containers (see pages 8–9). Leave to cool, then seal, label and date (see page 9) before freezing.

Microwave on high for 3 minutes, then remove from the microwave and stir. Re-cover but don't seal and microwave for a further 5 minutes or until piping hot. Leave to stand for 3 minutes before serving.

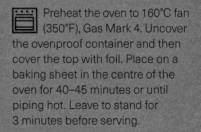 Preheat the oven to 160°C fan (350°F), Gas Mark 4. Uncover the ovenproof container and then cover the top with foil. Place on a baking sheet in the centre of the oven for 40–45 minutes or until piping hot. Leave to stand for 3 minutes before serving.

Spinach & ricotta cannelloni

This dish is a great way to feed a crowd and will no doubt become a family favourite. We have had it on the ByRuby menu since day one and it will stay there. Try serving it with a crisp green salad.

Similarly to our Slowly Braised Beef Ragu with Pappardelle Pasta (see page 70), this dish is fantastic when coupled with a fresh green salad. Think firm Little Gem leaves torn apart and tossed together with rocket or pea shoots, plus some fragrant herbs, such as chopped coriander, parsley or chives. Ready-prepared bags of mixed herby salad from the supermarket are a great choice for convenience. And why not quarter some radishes to add peppery piquancy, or shave over some raw carrot ribbons for added crunch? Our Classic Vinaigrette (see page 145) is the perfect dressing for your salad.

Makes 10–12 portions

about 500g (1lb 2oz) dried cannelloni pasta tubes
grated zest of 1 lemon

For the tomato sauce:
vegetable oil
1 large onion, finely chopped
2 carrots, finely chopped
3 celery sticks, finely chopped
4 garlic cloves, crushed
3 thyme sprigs, leaves picked and finely chopped, plus extra for sprinkling
4 rosemary sprigs, leaves picked and finely chopped
1 teaspoon dried oregano
2 fresh bay leaves
1 tablespoon tomato purée
2 × 400g (14oz) cans chopped tomatoes
1 teaspoon salt
15g (½oz) basil, leaves picked and roughly chopped

1 For the tomato sauce, heat a large, heavy-based pan over a low heat. Add a good glug of vegetable oil and then the onion and sweat for about 10 minutes until soft and translucent.

2 Add the carrots and celery and cook for about 5–10 minutes until softened. Then add the garlic, thyme, rosemary, oregano and bay leaves and cook for a futher 5 minutes.

3 Stir in the tomato purée, tomatoes and salt and simmer for 25–35 minutes, stirring occasionally, until the sauce has thickened. Remove from the heat, remove and discard the bay leaves and stir through the basil.

4 For the filling, squeeze out all the excess water from the defrosted spinach. Add to a food processor or blender with all the remaining filling ingredients and blitz until smooth.

5 Transfer the filling to a piping bag with a spoon ready to pipe into the cannelloni tubes.

6 If eating now, preheat the oven to 180°C fan (400°F), Gas Mark 6.

7 For the white sauce, melt the butter in a saucepan over a low heat, stir in the flour until the mixture forms a roux and cook for about 5 minutes, stirring constantly. Then gradually add the milk, a little at a time, whisking constantly until it is all incorporated and the sauce is smooth and thick. Remove from the heat and stir in the cheeses, nutmeg and mustard. Season to taste.

Continued overleaf ...

For the filling:

500g (1lb 2oz) frozen spinach leaves, defrosted
750g (1lb 10oz) ricotta cheese
50g (1¾oz) Parmesan cheese, finely grated
1 teaspoon freshly grated nutmeg
1 teaspoon pepper
1 teaspoon dried oregano
1 teaspoon salt

For the white sauce:

50g (1¾oz) unsalted butter
50g (1¾oz) plain flour
500ml (18fl oz) milk
50g (1¾oz) Parmesan cheese, finely grated
50g (1¾oz) Cheddar cheese, grated
1 teaspoon freshly grated nutmeg
2 teaspoons Dijon mustard
salt and pepper

8 Pipe the filling into the cannelloni tubes and set aside.

9 To assemble, if eating now, make a layer of all the tomato sauce in the base of a large baking dish, or put about 150g (5½oz) of tomato sauce in the base of individual baking dishes. Add the filled cannelloni, about three tubes per individual dish, then top with a layer of white sauce, about 100g (3½oz) per individual dish. Sprinkle over the lemon zest and extra thyme leaves.

10 Bake for 35–40 minutes or until golden brown on top and piping hot.

Portion out as directed in step 9 (above) into individual freezer-safe and ovenproof containers or dishes (see pages 8–9). Leave to cool, then put the lids on or wrap tightly in clingfilm or foil, label and date (see page 9) before freezing.

Preheat the oven to 160°C fan (350°F), Gas Mark 4. Uncover the ovenproof container or dish and place on a baking sheet in the centre of the oven for 40–45 minutes or until golden brown on top and piping hot. Leave to stand for 3 minutes before serving.

Cauliflower korma

This really tastes just like your favourite Indian takeaway korma. It's rich sauce is something you will crave and keep coming back to for more, but you need not worry, as it isn't ladened with dairy cream, hard as it is to believe! Having a stash of this in your freezer will stop you reaching for that takeaway menu – perfect for a Friday night feast, served with one or two of the other ByRuby curries, Naan Breads (see page 148) and some rice.

Makes 10 portions **DF / GF / V / VE**

vegetable oil
2 large onions, roughly chopped
3 garlic cloves, finely chopped
3cm (1¼-inch) piece of fresh root ginger, peeled and roughly chopped
2 tablespoons tomato purée
2 teaspoons salt
½ tablespoon smoked paprika
½ tablespoon ground turmeric
1 teaspoon chilli powder
2 teaspoons ground coriander
2 teaspoons medium curry powder
2 large cauliflowers, cut into florets, stalks roughly chopped
2 tablespoons ground almonds
2 tablespoons desiccated coconut
1 teaspoon sugar
2 × 400ml (14fl oz) cans coconut milk
salt and pepper

To garnish (optional):

2 tablespoons flaked almonds, toasted
handful of fresh coriander leaves, roughly chopped

1 Heat a large, heavy-based pan over a medium heat. Add a good glug of vegetable oil and then the onions, garlic and ginger and cook for 5 minutes.

2 Cover the onion mixture with water and bring to the boil, then reduce the heat and simmer gently for 30–35 minutes, stirring occasionally, until most of the liquid has evaporated.

3 Stir in the tomato purée, salt and spices and cook for a further 10 minutes.

4 Meanwhile, preheat the oven to 180°C fan (400°F), Gas Mark 6.

5 Remove the pan from the heat and blitz with a hand blender or in a food processor or blender until smooth.

6 Mix one-third of the vegetable mixture with the cauliflower pieces on a baking tray, spread out and roast for 25 minutes or until the cauliflower is cooked through and slightly caramelized.

7 While the cauliflower is roasting, add the ground almonds, desiccated coconut and sugar to the remaining vegetable mixture in the pan and stir until the sugar has dissolved. Then stir in the coconut milk and continue to simmer over a medium–low heat for 15 minutes, stirring occasionally.

8 Remove from the heat and season to taste. Fold in the roasted cauliflower and serve, sprinkled with the toasted flaked almonds and chopped coriander leaves, if you like.

Portion out the Cauliflower Korma into appropriate containers (see pages 8–9). Leave to cool, then sprinkle with a few toasted flaked almonds, if you like. Seal, label and date (see page 9) before freezing.

Microwave on high for 3 minutes, then remove from the microwave and stir. Re-cover but don't seal and microwave for a further 5 minutes or until piping hot. Leave to stand for 3 minutes before serving.

Preheat the oven to 160°C fan (350°F), Gas Mark 4. Uncover the ovenproof container and then cover the top with foil. Place on a baking sheet in the centre of the oven for 40–45 minutes or until piping hot. Leave to stand for 3 minutes before serving.

Vegetable lasagne
with butternut squash & aubergine

Makes 8–10 portions **DF / V / VE**

vegetable oil
1 large onion, finely chopped
5 large carrots, diced
4 celery sticks, diced
3 garlic cloves, crushed
4 thyme sprigs, leaves picked and
    finely chopped
6 rosemary sprigs, leaves picked and
    finely chopped
1 teaspoon dried oregano
2 fresh bay leaves
1 tablespoon tomato purée
400g (14oz) can chopped tomatoes
15g (½oz) basil, leaves picked and chopped
1 butternut squash, peeled, deseeded and
    sliced into rounds 1cm (½ inch) thick
3 aubergines, sliced into rounds 1cm
    (½ inch) thick
olivo oil
250g (9oz) dried lasagne sheets
200g (7oz) baby spinach leaves
salt

For the white sauce:
180ml (6¼fl oz) vegetable oil
180g (6¼oz) plain flour
1 litre (1¾ pints) oat milk or other
    plant-based milk
1 teaspoon freshly grated nutmeg
1 teaspoon pepper
1 teaspoon salt
3 tablespoons nutritional yeast flakes
1 teaspoon cider vinegar

This lasagne is great for feeding a crowd and no one will guess it's vegan. The vegetables add a pleasing sweetness to the dish. Perfect served with a fresh green salad.

1 Heat a large, heavy-based pan over a low heat. Add a good glug of vegetable oil and then the onion and sweat for about 10 minutes until soft and translucent. Add the carrots and celery and cook for about 5 minutes until softened. Then add the garlic, thyme, half the rosemary, the oregano and bay leaves and cook for a further 2 minutes. Stir in the tomato purée and tomatoes and simmer for 30–35 minutes, stirring occasionally, until the sauce has thickened. Remove from the heat. Remove and discard the bay leaves, season to taste with salt and stir through the basil.

2 Meanwhile, preheat the oven to 180°C fan (400°F), Gas Mark 6. Line a large baking tray with nonstick baking paper.

3 Spread the butternut squash and aubergine slices out on the lined baking tray without overlapping, season with salt and sprinkle over the remaining rosemary. Drizzle with olive oil and roast for 15–20 minutes or until golden. If eating now, leave the oven on for baking the dish, but if freezing, turn it off.

4 For the white sauce, heat a saucepan over a low heat. Add the vegetable oil, stir in the flour until the mixture forms a roux and cook for about 5 minutes, stirring constantly. Then gradually add the milk, a little at a time, whisking constantly until it is all incorporated and the sauce is smooth and thick. Remove from the heat and stir in the nutmeg, pepper, salt, nutritional yeast and vinegar.

5 To assemble, put a layer of tomato sauce in the base of a baking dish, followed by a layer of roasted squash and aubergine, then a layer of lasagne and a layer of white sauce and a layer of baby spinach. Repeat the layers until you have used up all the ingredients, finishing with a layer of white sauce. If eating now, bake for 35–40 minutes or until golden brown on top and piping hot.

❄ Portion out the lasagne into freezer-safe and ovenproof containers or dishes (see pages 8–9). Leave to cool, then put the lids on or wrap tightly in clingfilm or foil, label and date (see page 9) before freezing.

▦ Preheat the oven to 160°C fan (350°F), Gas Mark 4. Uncover the ovenproof container or dish and place on a baking sheet in the centre of the oven for 40–45 minutes or until golden brown on top and piping hot.

Leave to stand for 3 minutes before serving.

Ruby's greatest quiche

This is a great entertaining or picnic recipe, and a showstopper in its own right. Use the base recipe and then add whatever ingredients you like to the filling, depending on what's in season at the time or what you have to use up in the refrigerator. I have given a few ideas here, but there really are few limits to what you can add.

Makes one 23cm (9-inch) square or 25cm (10-inch) round quiche or 8 individual quiches

For the quiche base:

800g (1lb 12oz) shortcrust pastry, in a block or ready-rolled
plain flour, for dusting, if needed
5 eggs
500ml (18fl oz) double cream
generous handful of finely grated Cheddar cheese or Parmesan cheese
1 teaspoon freshly grated nutmeg
salt and pepper

1 Preheat the oven to 180°C fan (400°F), Gas Mark 6.

2 Roll the pastry out on a lightly floured work surface, if not using ready-rolled, large enough to line a 23cm (9-inch) square or 25cm (10-inch) round fluted tart tin, or cut out rounds large enough to line eight individual fluted tart tins. Lay the pastry over the tin(s) and press it gently into the corners and sides, leaving a little excess pastry around the edge of the tin(s) to allow for shrinkage during baking. Line the pastry case/cases with nonstick baking paper and weigh down with baking beans.

3 Bake the large pastry case for about 15 minutes, or bake the individual pastry cases for about 10 minutes, or until the sides are pale golden brown. Remove from the oven and lift out the paper and beans.

4 Beat the eggs with the remaining base ingredients in a bowl, then add your chosen filling ingredients (see opposite). Carefully pour the mixture into the baked pastry case(s).

5 Bake in the centre of the oven for 30–35 minutes for a large quiche, or 25–30 minutes for smaller individual quiches, until the filling is just set and golden but with a slight wobble in the middle. Serve warm.

Leave the quiche(s) to cool in the tin(s), then carefully remove. Place larger quiches on disposable cardboard silver cake bases before wrapping. Smaller quiches should be wrapped individually in clingfilm. Label and date (see page 9) before freezing.

Defrost in the refrigerator overnight and serve cold or at room temperature.

To serve the defrosted quiche(s) warm, preheat the oven to 160°C fan (350°F), Gas Mark 4. Unwrap the quiche(s) and place on a baking sheet in the centre of the oven for 30–35 minutes for a large quiche, or 25–30 minutes for smaller individual quiches, until piping hot. Leave to cool for a few minutes before serving.

For spinach, thyme & mushroom filling:

500g (1lb 2oz) spinach leaves, rinsed and cooked briefly in a pan with just the water clinging to the leaves until wilted, then excess water squeezed out

3 thyme sprigs, leaves picked and finely chopped

250g (9oz) chestnut mushrooms, sliced, then cooked in a little vegetable oil

For courgette, lemon & dill filling:

2 large courgettes, coarsely grated, sprinkled with salt and left to drain for 10 minutes, then rinsed, drained and excess water squeezed out

grated zest of 2 lemons

15g (½oz) dill, finely chopped

100g (3½oz) feta cheese, crumbled (optional)

For three-cheese & leek filling:

3 large leeks, trimmed, cleaned and finely chopped, then sweated in a little vegetable oil until soft

100g (3½oz) taleggio cheese, chopped

100g (3½oz) Cheddar cheese, grated

1 ball of mozzarella cheese, 125g (4½oz) drained weight, chopped

For Mediterranean roasted vegetable filling:

1 courgette, roughly chopped and roasted

1 red onion, roughly chopped and roasted

1 red pepper, cored, deseeded and roughly chopped, then roasted

1 yellow pepper, cored, deseeded and roughly chopped, then roasted

15g (½oz) basil, leaves picked and roughly chopped

4 thyme sprigs, leaves picked and roughly chopped

For red onion marmalade & goats' cheese filling:

200g (7oz) red onion marmalade

100g (3½oz) goats' cheese, crumbled

4 thyme sprigs, leaves picked and roughly chopped

For asparagus, pea & spring herb filling:

1 bunch of asparagus, about 250g (9oz), trimmed and thick stalks cut into rounds, tips kept whole

200g (7oz) frozen peas

small handful each of flat leaf parsley, tarragon, basil and mint, leaves picked and roughly chopped

For roasted fennel, mozzarella cheese & parsley filling:

3 fennel bulbs, quartered and roasted

1 ball of mozzarella, 125g (4½oz) drained weight, roughly chopped

15g (½oz) flat leaf parsley, leaves picked and roughly chopped

For tomato, pesto & ricotta filling:

250g (9oz) cherry tomatoes, halved

50g (1¾oz) pesto (see page 140 for homemade)

200g (7oz) ricotta cheese

finely grated Parmesan cheese, to serve (optional)

Mushroom stroganoff

This is a delicious version of the classic beef dish, which I personally prefer to the original. Packed full of flavour, it will brighten up your day. You can serve it with rice or pasta, or just on its own with some greens.

Makes 6–8 portions

50g (1¾oz) dried porcini mushrooms
250ml (9fl oz) water
25g (1oz) unsalted butter
1 tablespoon vegetable oil
2 onions, sliced
4 thyme sprigs, leaves picked and
    finely chopped
2 garlic cloves, crushed
1 tablespoon smoked paprika
6 Portobello mushrooms, sliced about
    5mm (¼ inch) thick
1 vegetable stock cube
1 teaspoon Marmite
3 tablespoons soured cream
50ml (2fl oz) double cream
1 tablespoon Dijon mustard
1 teaspoon lemon juice
15g (½oz) flat leaf parsley, leaves picked and
    roughly chopped, plus extra to garnish
salt and pepper
handful of finely grated Parmesan cheese,
    to serve

1 Put the dried mushrooms into a pan, cover with the measured water and bring to the boil over a medium heat. Remove from the heat and leave the mushrooms to soak for 5–10 minutes or until rehydrated. Strain the liquid into a jug and reserve. Roughly chop the mushrooms and set aside.

2 While the mushrooms are soaking, melt the butter with the vegetable oil in a large, heavy-based pan over a medium heat. Add the onions with 1 teaspoon of salt and sweat for about 10 minutes until soft and translucent (take your time with this – it really makes the dish!).

3 Add the thyme, garlic and smoked paprika and cook for 2 minutes, stirring frequently. Then add the Portobello mushrooms.

4 Stir in the rehydrated mushrooms and their soaking liquid and crumble in the stock cube. Simmer for about 15 minutes, stirring occasionally, until the liquid has reduced by half.

5 Remove from the heat and stir in the Marmite, soured cream, cream, mustard and lemon juice. Season to taste.

6 Stir in the parsley and serve sprinkled with the extra chopped parsley and the grated Parmesan.

Portion out the mushroom mixture into appropriate containers (see pages 8–9). Leave to cool, then seal, label and date (see page 9) before freezing.

Microwave on high for 3 minutes, then remove from the microwave and stir. Re-cover but don't seal and microwave for a further 5 minutes or until piping hot. Leave to stand for 3 minutes before serving.

Preheat the oven to 160°C fan (350°F), Gas Mark 4. Uncover the ovenproof container and then cover the top with foil. Place on a baking sheet in the centre of the oven for 40–45 minutes or until piping hot. Leave to stand for 3 minutes before serving.

Three greens seasonal filo pie

This is my very loose take on the Greek pie spanakopita. Packed with fresh herbs and feta, it's a vegetarian feast and a great way to use up green vegetables – swap out those specified here for what's in season or what you have in stock. Delicious served with a crisp green salad or some of our Super-easy Rosemary & Garlic Roast Potatoes (see page 119).

Makes 8-10 portions **VE** (if made with vegetarian feta)

vegetable oil
3 red onions, finely chopped
2 garlic cloves, crushed
2 teaspoons dried oregano
1 teaspoon freshly grated nutmeg
1 teaspoon ground cumin
1 teaspoon ground coriander
4 courgettes, coarsely grated
200g (7oz) chard, roughly chopped
200g (7oz) baby spinach leaves,
    roughly chopped
15g (½oz) flat leaf parsley, leaves
    picked and roughly chopped
10g (¼oz) dill, leaves picked and
    roughly chopped
10g (¼oz) mint, leaves picked and
    roughly chopped
250g (9oz) feta cheese, crumbled
about 10–12 filo pastry sheets
20g (¾oz) unsalted butter, melted

1 If eating now, preheat the oven to 180°C fan (400°F), Gas Mark 6.

2 Heat a pan over a low heat. Add a glug of vegetable oil and then the onions and sweat for about 10 minutes until soft and translucent.

3 Stir in the garlic, oregano and spices and cook for 5 minutes, stirring frequently.

4 Add the courgettes, chard and spinach and cook for a further 5 minutes.

5 Remove from the heat and stir in the herbs and feta.

6 If you are eating now, place the feta mixture in a deep baking dish. Brush each filo pastry sheet in turn lightly with melted butter, then scrunch up and place on top of the feta mixture until evenly covered.

7 Bake for 30–35 minutes or until the pastry is golden brown.

Portion out the feta mixture into freezer-safe and ovenproof containers or dishes (see pages 8–9) and leave to cool, then top with the scrunched-up buttered filo pastry as above. Put the lids on or wrap tightly in clingfilm or foil, label and date (see page 9) before freezing.

Preheat the oven to 160°C fan (350°F), Gas Mark 4. Uncover the ovenproof container or dish, place on a baking sheet and bake for 40–45 minutes or until the pastry is golden brown and the filling is piping hot.

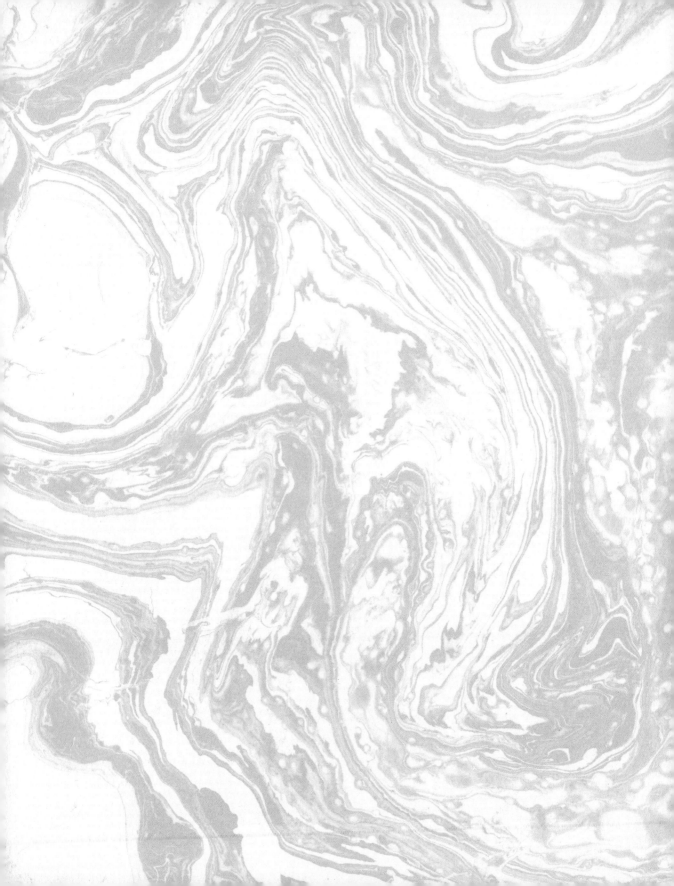

Family food
(from 6 months)

Cornflake chicken dippers

Who doesn't love chicken dippers? I like to use chicken thigh fillets, as the meat stays juicer when cooked and frozen. I always love to add a bit of extra flavour even when cooking for the children – a bit of garlic here, a touch of mustard there – as it makes things more interesting for everyone. These chicken dippers are suitable for children aged about 10 months or older, and they can be chopped up into very small pieces for those who don't yet have teeth.

Makes about 18 dippers

300ml (10fl oz) full-fat natural yogurt
1 garlic clove, crushed
1 teaspoon Dijon mustard, plus extra (optional) to serve
1 teaspoon maple syrup
6 boneless, skinless chicken thighs, each sliced into about 3 strips
100g (3½oz) cornflakes
50g (1¾oz) flaked almonds
olive oil

1 Mix the yogurt, garlic, mustard and maple syrup together in a large bowl.

2 Add the chicken strips and stir to coat. Cover and leave to marinate in the refrigerator for about an hour, or longer if you have the time (but no more than 12 hours in total).

3 Put the cornflakes and almonds into a freezer bag, seal securely and bash with a rolling pin until crushed. Transfer the cornflake mixture to a large shallow bowl.

4 Preheat the oven to 200°C fan (425°F), Gas Mark 7. Line a baking tray with nonstick baking paper and brush with olive oil.

5 Dip each chicken strip into the cornflake mixture to coat completely, then transfer to the prepared baking tray.

6 Once all the chicken is coated, drizzle with olive oil and bake for 25 minutes until crispy and golden brown.

7 Serve with extra Dijon mustard for dipping, if you like.

Leave the chicken dippers to cool, then put into freezer bags, making sure they are laid out flat in each bag, side by side, so that they don't stick together when frozen. Seal, label and date (see page 9) before freezing.

Preheat the oven to 160°C fan (350°F), Gas Mark 4. Place the frozen chicken dippers on a baking tray lined with nonstick baking paper and bake for about 20 minutes or until heated through.

Fishcakes

This recipe was inspired by the wonderful Chiappa sisters and their book *Baby at the Table* – think healthy alternative to fish fingers. They go down well with all children and are brilliant for feeding the whole family in a jiffy. Although a complete meal in themselves, I often poach an egg to go on top or make a quick green salad for the perfect midweek dinner.

Makes 12 fishcakes (2 per adult portion)

olive oil
250g (9oz) sweet potato, peeled and cut into 1cm (½-inch) cubes
250g (9oz) skinless salmon or trout fillets, cut into 2cm (¾-inch) chunks, any stray bones removed
100g (3½oz) frozen peas
500ml (18fl oz) milk
grated zest of 1 lemon
2 eggs, beaten
100g (3½oz) panko breadcrumbs or slightly stale white bread blitzed to crumbs in a food processor, or crushed cornflakes
salt and pepper

1 Preheat the oven to 180°C fan (400°F), Gas Mark 6. Brush a baking tray with olive oil.

2 Put the sweet potato, fish and peas into a pan and cover with the milk. Bring to a simmer and cook for 10 minutes or until the sweet potato is soft and the fish is cooked through.

3 Drain off the milk and transfer the sweet potato, fish and pea mixture to a bowl. Mash with a potato masher, leaving a bit of texture to the fish, and leave to cool slightly. If catering for a baby, remove a portion and blitz to a purée with a hand blender or in a blender to the appropriate consistency.

4 Add the lemon zest and half the beaten egg to the remaining fish mixture and mix together. Season with salt and pepper.

5 Divide the fish mixture into 10 (if you've removed some for the baby) or 12 even-sized portions and form into patties about 2cm (¾ inch) thick.

6 Put the remaining beaten egg into a shallow bowl and put the breadcrumbs or cornflakes into a separate one.

7 Dip each fishcake in turn into the beaten egg and then toss in the breadcrumbs or cornflakes until well coated. Place on the oiled baking tray.

8 Drizzle the fishcakes with olive oil and bake for 20 minutes until golden brown, then serve hot.

❄ Leave the fishcakes to cool, then portion out into freezer bags. Seal, label and date (see page 9) before freezing. Portion out the cooled purée for a baby into an ice-cube tray. The frozen cubes can then be popped out directly into a labelled freezer bag.

Transfer frozen cubes of purée to a covered microwave-safe container. Microwave on high for 1 minute, then remove from the microwave and stir. Re-cover but don't seal and microwave for a further 1–2 minutes. Leave to stand until cooled to the appropriate temperature before serving.

Preheat the oven to 160°C fan (350°F), Gas Mark 4. Place the frozen fishcakes on a lined baking tray in the centre of the oven for 20–25 minutes until hot.

Heat frozen cubes of purée in a small pan over a low heat for 5 minutes or until piping hot, stirring.

Best-ever macaroni cheese

This is hands down the best macaroni cheese recipe out there. It works well heated directly from frozen and is a sure-fire crowd-pleaser. The topping adds an extra dimension of uber-cheesy comfort. Add cooked bacon or mushrooms to the recipe if you like, but I love it as it is. And don't fear the addition of Dijon mustard for children – mine love it! Miniature star pasta (stellette) works brilliantly for babies instead of macaroni. This is suitable for babies from about 10 months.

Makes 8–10 adult-sized portions

1kg (2lb 4oz) dried macaroni pasta

For the sauce:
300g (10½oz) unsalted butter
300g (10½oz) plain flour
2.5 litres (4½ pints) milk
130g (4¾oz) Parmesan cheese, grated
130g (4¾oz) Cheddar cheese, grated
1 teaspoon freshly grated nutmeg
1 teaspoon salt
1 teaspoon pepper
600ml (20fl oz) double cream
1½ tablespoons Dijon mustard
1 tablespoon Worcestershire sauce
   (optional)

For the topping:
30g (1oz) unsalted butter
300g (10½oz) Cheddar cheese, grated
130g (4¾oz) Parmesan cheese, grated
1 tablespoon plain flour
½ tablespoon Dijon mustard
500ml (18fl oz) milk

1 Cook the pasta in a large pan of boiling water according to the packet instructions, for about 8–9 minutes, until al dente.

2 Meanwhile, for the sauce, melt the butter in a large saucepan over a low heat, stir in the flour until the mixture forms a roux and cook for about 5 minutes, stirring constantly. Then gradually add the milk, a little at a time, whisking constantly until it is all incorporated and the sauce is smooth and thick.

3 Remove from the heat and stir in the remaining sauce ingredients.

4 Drain the pasta and then mix with the sauce.

5 Put all the topping ingredients into a saucepan and heat over a low heat, whisking constantly, until the mixture is smooth and thickened, then remove from the heat. If the sauce is lumpy, quickly blitz it with a hand blender.

6 If eating now, preheat the grill to medium–high (200°C/400°F).

7 Transfer the macaroni mixture to a deep baking dish, then cover with the topping mixture, place under the hot grill and cook for 5–10 minutes or until golden brown on top. Leave to stand for 3 minutes before serving.

 Portion out the macaroni mixture into freezer-safe and ovenproof containers or dishes (see pages 8–9) and cover each portion with 100g (3½oz) of the topping mixture. Leave to cool, then put the lids on or wrap tightly in clingfilm or foil, label and date (see page 9) before freezing.

Preheat the oven to 160°C fan (350°F), Gas Mark 4. Uncover the ovenproof container or dish, place on a baking sheet and bake for 40–45 minutes or until golden brown on top and the filling is piping hot.

Apricot chicken tagine

It's important to include spices in children's diets from a young age. This tagine is warming and mildly spiced with the dried apricots giving a tempering sweetness. If you're a spice nut like me, add some chilli flakes when serving. Couscous makes an ideal accompaniment along with some green vegetables.

Makes 6 adult-sized portions **DF / GF**

vegetable oil
12 boneless, skinless chicken thighs
1 large onion, diced
2 garlic cloves, sliced
1 teaspoon grated fresh root ginger
1 teaspoon ground coriander
1 teaspoon ground cumin
1 sweet potato, peeled and grated
1 carrot, peeled and grated
6 dried apricots, finely sliced
400g (14oz) can chopped tomatoes
500ml (18fl oz) hot chicken stock
    (low salt if cooking for children)
½ butternut squash, peeled, deseeded
    and cut into 1cm (½-inch) cubes
salt and pepper
fresh coriander leaves, to garnish

1 Heat a large, heavy-based pan with a lid over a high heat and pour in enough vegetable oil to cover the base. Add the chicken thighs, in batches to avoid overcrowding the pan, and brown on both sides. Set aside on a plate.

2 Add a little more oil to the pan and then the onion and garlic and sweat over a low heat for 10 minutes until soft and translucent.

3 Add the ginger, ground coriander and cumin and cook until aromatic, stirring frequently. Then stir in the sweet potato and carrot until coated in the spice mixture. Reduce the heat to low, cover the pan with the lid and sweat for a further 10 minutes.

4 Add the apricots, pour in the tomatoes and stock and stir in the butternut squash, followed by the chicken with any juices on the plate. Replace the lid and simmer for about 40 minutes, stirring occasionally, until the chicken is cooked through and tender and the squash is soft. If you prefer, you can cook the tagine in an ovenproof dish with a lid in a preheated oven at 160°C fan (350°F), Gas Mark 4.

5 If catering for a baby, remove a portion of the tagine and blitz with a hand blender or in a blender to the appropriate consistency. Season the remaining mixture to taste, garnish with coriander leaves and serve.

Portion out the chicken tagine mixture into appropriate containers (see pages 8–9), or ice-cube trays for convenient-sized portions of the purée for a baby. Leave to cool, then seal, label and date (see page 9) before freezing. If freezing in ice-cube trays, the frozen cubes can then be popped out directly into labelled freezer bags.

Microwave on high for 3 minutes, then remove from the microwave and stir. Re-cover but don't seal and microwave for a further 5 minutes or until piping hot. Leave to stand for 3 minutes before serving. Transfer frozen cubes to a covered microwave-safe container. Microwave as before but for 2–3 minutes in total, stirring about halfway through. Leave to cool to the appropriate temperature before serving.

Preheat the oven to 160°C fan (350°F), Gas Mark 4. Uncover the ovenproof container and then cover the top with foil. Place on a baking sheet in the centre of the oven for 40–45 minutes or until piping hot. Leave to stand for 3 minutes before serving.

Heat frozen cubes in a small pan over a low heat for 5 minutes or until hot, stirring. Leave to cool to the appropriate temperature before serving.

Beef & sweet potato stew

A tasty winter warmer, this stew is great served with rice but I also love it with orzo pasta topped with a sprinkling of grated Parmesan cheese. Adding the harissa at the end peps it up nicely if you like things spicy like me.

Makes 6 adult-sized portions **DF**

vegetable oil
1kg (2lb 4oz) stewing beef, such as chuck, cut into 2cm (¾-inch) chunks
1 large onion, diced
2 garlic cloves, sliced
3 carrots, diced
1 teaspoon dried mixed herbs
2 tablespoons plain flour
1 litre (1¾ pints) hot beef stock (low salt if cooking for children)
1 tablespoon tomato purée
1 fresh or dried bay leaf
3 sweet potatoes, peeled and cut into 2cm (¾-inch) chunks
olive oil
1 tablespoon rose harissa (optional)
salt and pepper
Flatbreads (see page 146), to serve (optional)

1 Heat a large, heavy-based pan with a lid over a high heat and add a good glug of vegetable oil. Then add the beef, in batches to avoid overcrowding the pan, and brown all over. Set aside on a plate.

2 Add another glug of vegetable oil to the pan and then the onion, garlic and carrots with the dried mixed herbs and sweat over a low heat for about 10 minutes until the onion is soft and translucent.

3 Return the beef to the pan with any meat juices on the plate, sprinkle over the flour and stir until the beef and vegetables are coated. Gradually add the stock and then the tomato purée and bay leaf, stirring constantly. Bring to a simmer, then reduce the heat, put the lid on the pan and simmer gently for an hour or until the beef is falling apart, stirring occasionally and adding a little water if the stew is too thick. Remove and discard the bay leaf.

4 Meanwhile, preheat the oven to 180°C fan (400°F), Gas Mark 6.

5 Spread the sweet potato chunks out on a baking tray, drizzle with olive oil and roast for 30 minutes or until cooked through.

6 Once the beef is done, stir the roasted sweet potato chunks through the stew. If catering for a baby, remove a portion of the stew and blitz with a hand blender or in a blender to the appropriate consistency. Stir the harissa into the remaining mixture, if using, then season to taste. Serve with flatbreads, if you like.

Portion out the stew into appropriate containers (see pages 8–9), or ice-cube trays for convenient-sized portions of the purée for a baby. Leave to cool, then seal, label and date (see page 9) before freezing. If freezing in ice-cube trays, the frozen cubes can then be popped out directly into labelled freezer bags.

 Microwave on high for 3 minutes, then remove from the microwave and stir. Re-cover but don't seal and microwave for a further 5 minutes or until piping hot. Leave to stand for 3 minutes before serving. Transfer frozen cubes to a covered microwave-safe container. Microwave as before but for 2–3 minutes in total, stirring about halfway through. Leave to cool to the appropriate temperature before serving.

 Preheat the oven to 160°C fan (350°F), Gas Mark 4. Uncover the ovenproof container and then cover the top with foil. Place on a baking sheet in the centre of the oven for about 40–45 minutes or until piping hot. Leave to stand for 3 minutes before serving.

Heat frozen cubes in a pan over a low heat for 5 minutes or until piping hot, stirring. Leave to cool to the appropriate temperature before serving.

Veg-packed Bolognaise

However much I would love to say that my children eat everything, there are times when vegetables don't always go down best in their raw form. This Bolognaise sauce is a stalwart in my freezer and is a perfect way of sneakily including veg for those who are sometimes a little averse. This recipe is so versatile – you can stir in some harissa to make a chilli or turn it into a cottage pie by topping with mashed potato (see page 113). Otherwise, serve it the traditional way with pasta for a meal everyone in the family will enjoy.

Makes 8 adult-sized portions **DF / GF**

olive oil
1 large onion, diced
1 garlic clove, crushed
1 celery stick, finely diced
½ teaspoon dried mixed herbs
250g (9oz) sweet potatoes, peeled
   and coarsely grated
250g (9oz) courgettes, coarsely grated
500g (1lb 2oz) minced beef
1 litre (1¾ pints) hot beef stock (low salt
   if cooking for children)
2 × 400g (14oz) cans chopped tomatoes
salt and pepper

1 Heat a large, heavy-based pan over a low heat. Add a good glug of olive oil and then the onion, garlic and celery with the dried mixed herbs and sweat for about 5 minutes until translucent.

2 Add the sweet potatoes and courgettes and cook for 10 minutes until softened.

3 Turn the heat up, add the minced beef, season, and cook, breaking it up with a wooden spoon, until it has all browned.

4 Pour in the stock and tomatoes and bring to a simmer. Reduce the heat and simmer gently for about an hour, stirring occasionally.

5 If catering for a baby, remove a portion and blitz with a hand blender or in a blender to the appropriate consistency. Season the remaining mixture to taste, then serve.

Portion out the sauce into appropriate containers (see pages 8–9), or ice-cube trays for convenient-sized portions of the purée for a baby. Leave to cool, then seal, label and date (see page 9) before freezing. If freezing in ice-cube trays, the frozen cubes can then be popped out directly into labelled freezer bags.

Microwave on high for 3 minutes, then remove from the microwave and stir. Re-cover but don't seal and microwave for a further 3 minutes or until piping hot. Leave to stand for 3 mintues before serving. Transfer frozen cubes to a covered microwave-safe container. Microwave as before but for 2–3 minutes in total, stirring about halfway through. Leave to cool to the appropriate temperature before serving.

Preheat the oven to 160°C fan (350°F), Gas Mark 4. Uncover the ovenproof container and then cover the top with foil. Place on a baking sheet in the centre of the oven for 25–30 minutes or until piping hot. Leave to stand for 3 minutes before serving.

Heat frozen cubes in a pan over a low heat for 5 minutes or until piping hot, stirring. Leave to cool to the appropriate temperature before serving.

Kiddie korma

For as long as I can remember, I have always loved curry, and I have tried to incorporate spices into my children's diet at a very early stage. This sauce is great on its own, but storing it in the freezer means you can pull it out whenever you need and pour it over some leftover roasted vegetables or cooked chicken or fish. I've kept it very mildly spiced, but you can add a sprinkling of chilli flakes to the finished sauce for those with a more fiery palate.

Makes about 8 adult-sized portions
DF / GF / V / VE

vegetable oil
1 large onion, finely chopped
1 garlic clove, finely chopped
1 thumb-sized piece of fresh root ginger, peeled and finely chopped
1 teaspoon ground turmeric
1 teaspoon garam masala
½ teaspoon ground cumin
½ teaspoon ground coriander
250g (9oz) butternut squash, peeled, deseeded and diced
250g (9oz) carrots, diced
4 dried apricots, chopped
400g (14oz) can chopped tomatoes
250ml (9fl oz) hot vegetable stock (low salt if cooking for children)
400ml (14fl oz) can coconut milk
salt and pepper

1 Heat a large, heavy-based pan over a medium heat. Add a good glug of vegetable oil and then add the onion, garlic and ginger and sweat for about 5 minutes until translucent.

2 Add the ground spices to the pan and cook for about 2 minutes until aromatic, stirring frequently.

3 Add the butternut squash, carrots and apricots and stir for 2 minutes until well coated in the spices.

4 Pour in the tomatoes and stock along with a little water if necessary to cover the vegetables. Simmer for about 25–30 minutes, stirring occasionally, until the vegetables are cooked through.

5 Blitz with a hand blender or in a food processor or blender until smooth, then return the blended mixture to the pan.

6 Stir in the coconut milk. If catering for a baby, remove a portion, then season the remaining mixure to taste, heat through and serve.

Portion out the korma into appropriate containers (see pages 8–9), or ice-cube trays for convenient-sized portions for a baby. Leave to cool, then seal and label (see page 9) before freezing. If freezing in ice-cube trays, the frozen cubes can then be popped out into labelled freezer bags.

Microwave on high for 3 minutes, then remove from the microwave and stir. Re-cover but don't seal and microwave for a further 3 minutes or until hot. Leave to stand for 3 mintues before serving. Transfer frozen cubes to a covered microwave-safe container. Microwave as before but for 2–3 minutes in total, stirring about halfway through. Leave to stand until cooled to the appropriate temperature before serving.

Preheat the oven to 160°C fan (350°F), Gas Mark 4. Uncover the ovenproof container and then cover the top with foil. Place on a baking sheet in the centre of the oven for 25–30 minutes or until piping hot. Leave to stand for 3 minutes before serving.

Heat frozen cubes in a pan over a low heat for 5 minutes or until piping hot, stirring. Leave to cool to the appropriate temperature before serving.

Pork, courgette & Parmesan meatballs

These meatballs are completely delicious, and a mainstay of my freezer for children and adults alike. Add to our Super-duper Tomato Sauce (see page 139) and serve with pasta or enjoy them on their own with some veggies and fries. Broken up or blended into tomato sauce with rice or tiny pasta, these are great for babies during the early finger food days, from about 10 months.

Makes 6 adult-sized portions

vegetable oil
1 onion, finely diced
1 garlic clove, crushed
1 teaspoon fennel seeds
500g (1lb 2oz) minced pork
500g (1lb 2oz) courgettes, coarsely grated
100g (3½oz) fresh or dried breadcrumbs
  (you can use any kind of bread)
75g (2¾oz) Parmesan cheese, finely grated
1 chicken stock cube, dissolved in 50ml
  (2fl oz) boiling water, then left to cool
2 eggs, beaten
salt and pepper

1 Preheat the oven to 200°C fan (425°F), Gas Mark 7. Line a baking tray with nonstick baking paper and brush with vegetable oil.

2 Heat a frying pan over a low heat. Add 1 tablespoon of vegetable oil and then the onion with the garlic and fennel seeds and sweat for about 10 minutes until soft and translucent. Leave to cool.

3 Meanwhile, put all the remaining ingredients except the seasoning into a large bowl and knead together with your hands until well blended.

4 Mix the cooled onion mixture into the pork mixture. If catering for a baby, remove a portion and season the remaining mixture with salt and pepper. To check the seasoning, cook a little bit of the mixture in a pan, taste and adjust accordingly.

5 Roll the pork mixture into 3cm (1¼-inch) balls and lay on the prepared baking tray, making sure you remember which ones are for the baby. Bake for 20 minutes until golden and cooked through.

Open-freeze the cooled cooked meatballs on a tray, then transfer to freezer bags. Seal, label and date (see page 9) before freezing.

Place the frozen meatballs on a microwave-safe plate, uncovered, and microwave on high for 5 minutes until heated through. Leave to cool to the appropriate temperature before serving.

Preheat the oven to 160°C fan (350°F), Gas Mark 4. Place the frozen meatballs, spaced apart, on a baking tray and bake for 15–20 minutes until heated through. Leave to cool to the appropriate temperature before serving.

Quick & easy pizzas

Who doesn't love a pizza? These are really fun to make with the children and even better if you keep a few frozen for a super-quick tea after a busy day. Serve with some vegetable crudités for a bit of extra veggie goodness.

Makes 6 pizzas

6 English muffins
150g (5½oz) Super-duper Tomato Sauce (see page 139) or ready-made tomato pizza sauce
180g (6¼oz) Cheddar or mozzarella cheese, grated
toppings of your choice, such as:
 – cherry tomatoes
 – finely diced ham or slices torn into strips
 – finely sliced cooked mushrooms
 – fresh, canned or frozen sweetcorn kernels
 – courgette ribbons
 – fresh or frozen peas
 – canned, flaked tuna
 – pitted olives

1 If eating now, preheat the oven to 200°C fan (425°F), Gas Mark 7.

2 Split the muffins in half and lay insides-up on a baking sheet. Spread each half with ½ tablespoon of tomato sauce and sprinkle with the cheese.

3 If eating now, add the topping of your or your children's choice.

4 Bake for 5–10 minutes or until the cheese has melted.

Tightly wrap the unbaked muffin halves topped with the tomato sauce and cheese individually in clingfilm or foil. Label and date (see page 9) before freezing.

Preheat the oven to 160°C fan (350°F), Gas Mark 4. Unwrap the pizzas, lay on a baking sheet and add your chosen toppings. Bake for 10–15 minutes or until the cheese has melted.

Creamy veggie pasta bake

This dish is an absolute fail-safe in my household and a hit with children and adults alike. It's a great way of using up any vegetables, so feel free to swap what's listed to whatever you have hanging around in the refrigerator. If your children are fussy about the texture of vegetables, simply blend them with the cream cheese before stirring into the pasta. You can also add leftover cooked chicken, salmon or ham if you have it. This goes down really well at the weaning stage, from about 10 months, if you use tiny pasta shapes, which we call 'fairy pasta' in our house.

Makes 4 adult-sized portions

250g (9oz) dried pasta of your choice
olive oil
1 onion, finely diced
1 garlic clove, crushed
150g (5½oz) courgettes, coarsely grated
handful of frozen peas or ½ head of
    broccoli, finely chopped
2 generous tablespoons cream cheese
2 large handfuls of finely grated
    Parmesan cheese
salt and pepper

1 If eating now, preheat the oven to 160°C fan (350°F), Gas Mark 4.

2 Meanwhile, cook the pasta in a large pan of boiling water according to the packet instructions until al dente.

3 While the pasta is cooking, heat a large, heavy-based pan over a low heat. Add a good glug of olive oil and then the onion and garlic and sweat for about 5 minutes or until the onion is translucent.

4 Add the vegetables, turn the heat up and cook for about 5 minutes until they are softened and lightly browned, stirring frequently to ensure they don't burn.

5 Stir in about half a ladleful of the pasta cooking water, the cream cheese and a handful of the Parmesan. (If you wish, you can at this stage blitz the sauce with a hand blender or in a food processor or blender until smooth.)

6 Drain the pasta and then mix with the sauce. If catering for a baby, remove a portion, then season the remaining mixture to taste.

7 If eating now, transfer the seasoned pasta mixture to a baking dish and sprinkle with the remaining Parmesan. Bake for about 15–20 minutes until golden brown on top.

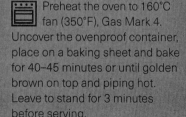

Portion out the seasoned pasta mixture into appropriate containers (see pages 8–9) and add a sprinkle of grated Parmesan. Leave to cool, then seal, label and date (see page 9) before freezing.

Microwave on high for 3 minutes, then remove from the microwave and stir. Re-cover but don't seal and microwave for a further 5 minutes or until piping hot. Leave to stand for 3 minutes before serving.

Preheat the oven to 160°C fan (350°F), Gas Mark 4. Uncover the ovenproof container, place on a baking sheet and bake for 40–45 minutes or until golden brown on top and piping hot. Leave to stand for 3 minutes before serving.

Classic chicken casserole

Packed full of veggies in addition to tender chicken, this casserole is a winner of a one-pot dish. Serve it with hunks of baguette for mopping up the delicious sauce.

Makes 6 adult-sized portions **DF**

vegetable oil
12 boneless, skinless chicken thighs
1 large onion, diced
2 garlic cloves, sliced
2 leeks, trimmed, cleaned and sliced
2 tablespoons plain flour
1 litre (1¾ pints) hot chicken stock
   (low salt if cooking for children)
350g (12oz) new potatoes, halved
3 carrots, sliced
1 fresh bay leaf
3 thyme sprigs
salt and pepper

1 Heat a large, heavy-based pan with a lid over a high heat and add a good glug of vegetable oil. Then add the chicken thighs, in batches to avoid overcrowding the pan, and brown on both sides. Set aside on a plate.

2 Add another glug of oil to the pan and then the onion, garlic and leeks and sweat over a low heat for about 10 minutes until the onion is soft and translucent.

3 Sprinkle over the flour and stir until the vegetables are coated. Then gradually add the stock, stirring constantly.

4 Return the chicken to the pan with any juices on the plate and stir in the potatoes, carrots and herbs. Bring to a simmer, then reduce the heat, put the lid on the pan and simmer gently for 40 minutes or until the chicken is very tender and the vegetables are cooked through, stirring occasionally and adding a little water if the sauce is too thick. Remove and discard the bay leaf and thyme sprigs.

5 If catering for a baby, remove a portion and blitz with a hand blender or in a blender to the appropriate consistency. Season the remaining mixture to taste.

Portion out the chicken mixture into appropriate containers (see pages 8–9), or ice-cube trays for convenient-sized portions of the purée for a baby. Leave to cool, then seal, label and date (see page 9) before freezing. If freezing in ice-cube trays, the frozen cubes can then be popped out into labelled freezer bags.

Microwave on high for 3 minutes, then remove from the microwave and stir. Re-cover but don't seal and microwave for a further 5 minutes or until piping hot. Leave to stand for 3 minutes before serving. Transfer frozen cubes to a covered microwave-safe container. Microwave as before but for 2–3 minutes in total, stirring about halfway through. Leave to cool to the appropriate temperature before serving.

Preheat the oven to 160°C fan (350°F), Gas Mark 4. Uncover the ovenproof container and then cover the top with foil. Place on a baking sheet in the centre of the oven for about 40–45 minutes or until piping hot. Leave to stand for 3 minutes before serving.

Heat frozen cubes in a pan over a low heat for 5 minutes or until piping hot, stirring. Leave to cool to the appropriate temperature before serving.

Mini savoury frittata bites

These work brilliantly as a canapé for grown-ups or as a wholesome and delicious meal for children or babies from about 10 months, and make a tasty addition to a picnic. They are a great way of using up leftovers in your refrigerator, such as roasted or fresh vegetables or ham and cheese. I use a mini muffin tin to make them easy for little fingers to cope with.

Makes 24 frittata bites **GF**

unsalted butter or vegetable oil, for greasing
150g (5½oz) frittata fillings of your choice, such as:
– grated uncooked courgette
– grated uncooked butternut squash
– finely diced uncooked peppers
– fresh or frozen uncooked peas
– fresh, canned or frozen sweetcorn kernels
– finely chopped roasted vegetables
– finely chopped cooked mushrooms
– finely chopped cooked potatoes
– finely diced ham
– finely diced roast chicken
– grated hard cheese, such as Cheddar
– crumbled goats' cheese
6 eggs
salt and pepper

1 Preheat the oven to 180°C fan (400°F), Gas Mark 6.

2 Grease a 24-hole silicone or tin mini muffin tray with butter or vegetable oil. Put around 1 teaspoon of the filling ingredient of your choice into each hole.

3 Beat the eggs together in a jug.

4 If catering for a baby, pour the egg mixture into as many muffin tray holes as you want for them.

5 Season the remaining egg mixture with salt and pepper and pour into the remaining holes.

6 Bake for 15–20 minutes or until the egg mixture is set. Serve warm or cool.

Leave to cool, then pop the frittatas out of the muffin tray directly into freezer bags, being careful not to overcrowd the bag. Seal, label and date (see page 9) before freezing.

Defrost in the refrigerator for 12 hours to serve cold.

 Place the frozen frittatas on a microwave-safe plate, uncovered, and microwave on high for 1–2 minutes or until heated through. Leave to stand for 1–2 minutes before serving.

Preheat the oven to 160°C fan (350°F), Gas Mark 4. Place the frozen frittatas on a baking sheet and bake for 10–15 minutes or until heated through.

Ruby's fabulous cottage pie

This family favourite is easy to make as a large batch. We add lots of fresh herbs to ours, but feel free to reduce these or take them out altogether if you prefer a more traditional version.

Makes 8–10 adult-sized portions **GF**

For the mashed potato topping:
3kg (6lb 8oz) potatoes, unpeeled
50g (1¾oz) unsalted butter, melted
1 teaspoon salt
1 teaspoon pepper

For the meat sauce:
vegetable oil
1 large onion, finely chopped
3 large carrots, finely chopped
3 celery sticks, finely chopped
3 garlic cloves, crushed
6 thyme sprigs, leaves picked and
    finely chopped
4 rosemary sprigs, leaves picked and
    finely chopped
½ tablespoon dried oregano
1kg (2lb 4oz) minced beef
1 beef stock cube (low salt if cooking
    for children)
1 tablespoon tomato purée
200ml (7fl oz) red wine or water
2 × 400g (14oz) cans chopped tomatoes
1 tablespoon Worcestershire sauce
1 tablespoon tomato ketchup
15g (½oz) flat leaf parsley, chopped
100g (3½oz) Cheddar cheese, grated
salt and pepper

1 Preheat the oven to 180°C fan (400°F), Gas Mark 6.

2 For the potato topping, place the potatoes on a baking tray and bake for about an hour until soft inside.

3 Meanwhile, for the meat sauce, heat a large, heavy-based pan over a medium heat. Add a good glug of vegetable oil and then the onion, carrots and celery and sweat for about 10 minutes until softened. Stir in the garlic, thyme, rosemary and oregano and cook for 5 minutes.

4 Add the minced beef, season, and cook, breaking it up with a wooden spoon, until it has all browned. Crumble in the stock cube and stir in with the tomato purée, then cook for 5 minutes.

5 Add the wine or water, tomatoes, Worcestershire sauce and ketchup and bring to a simmer. Reduce the heat and simmer for about 30–40 minutes, stirring occasionally, until the sauce is thick.

6 Once the baked potatoes are soft, allow them to cool then scoop out the insides into a bowl and crumble with your hands into small chunks or roughly mash with a potato masher or until smooth, depending on your preferred texture. Then mix in the melted butter, and salt and pepper (avoid salt if you are catering for a baby). If eating now, leave the oven on, but if freezing, turn it off.

7 When the meat sauce is ready, stir in the parsley.

8 If catering for a baby, combine a portion of the mince and potatoes and blitz with a hand blender or in a blender to the appropriate consistency. Freeze this in ice-cube trays, if you like.

9 If eating now, transfer the meat sauce to a large baking dish, cover with the potato topping and sprinkle with the grated Cheddar. Bake for 30–35 minutes until golden brown on top.

❄️ Portion out the meat sauce into appropriate containers (see pages 8–9), cover each portion with an equal quantity of the potato topping and add a sprinkle of grated Cheddar. Leave to cool, then seal, label and date (see page 9) before freezing.

🔲 Microwave on high for 3 minutes, then remove from the microwave and uncover. Re-cover but don't seal and microwave for a further 5 minutes or until piping hot. Leave to stand for 3 minutes before serving.

 Preheat the oven to 160°C fan (350°F), Gas Mark 4. Uncover the ovenproof container and place on a baking sheet in the centre of the oven for about 40–45 minutes or until golden brown on top and hot. Leave to stand for 3 minutes before serving.

Fridge-raid pilaf

Whenever I cook rice, I always do extra so that I can use it to make a quick and easy pilaf. In this recipe, I've added cooking instructions for the rice, but skip those if you have some leftover cooked rice – you'll need about 800g (1lb 12oz). This is a great way of using up any remnants of meat, fish or veggies in the refrigerator and it freezes brilliantly. The pilaf is suitable for babies from around 10 months as long as the ingredients are chopped finely.

Makes 6 adult-sized portions **DF / GF**

370g (13oz) basmati rice
750ml (1⅓ pints) water
1 tablespoon vegetable oil
1 onion, finely diced
1 garlic clove, crushed
½ teaspoon fennel seeds
150g (5½oz) uncooked or cooked meat or
    fish of your choice (cut into appropriately
    sized pieces), such as:
– uncooked pancetta or bacon
– leftover roast meat or fish
– smoked salmon or trout, or ham
200g (7oz) uncooked or cooked vegetables
    of your choice, such as:
– grated uncooked courgette, butternut
    squash, celeriac or sweet potato
– chopped uncooked peppers
– uncooked spinach leaves
– frozen peas, broad beans or spinach
– chopped roasted vegetables –
    courgettes, butternut squash, peppers
    or sweet potato
salt and pepper

1 Put the rice into a pan with a lid and pour over the measured water. Put the lid on the pan and bring to the boil, then reduce the heat and simmer for 8 minutes, without lifting the lid.

2 Meanwhile, heat a large frying pan, preferably with a lid, over a low heat. Add the vegetable oil and then the onion with the garlic and fennel seeds and sweat for about 10 minutes until soft and translucent.

3 Once the rice cooking time is up, turn the heat off, remove the lid and set aside, without stirring, for 5 minutes.

4 Add the pancetta or bacon, if using, to the onion, turn the heat up and cook for 5 minutes. Then add any uncooked or frozen vegetables and cook for 5 minutes, stirring frequently (if using frozen vegetables, put the lid on the pan if it has one).

5 If using cooked vegetables, meat or fish, or smoked salmon or trout or ham, add to the pan now and cook for a further 5 minutes.

6 Fluff the rice with a fork, then add to the pan and stir until combined and piping hot. If catering for a baby, remove a portion for the baby, then season the remaining mixture to taste.

 Portion out the rice mixture into appropriate containers (see pages 8–9). Leave to cool, then seal, label and date (see page 9) before freezing.

 Microwave on high for 3 minutes, then remove from the microwave and stir. Re-cover but don't seal and microwave for a further 3 minutes or until piping hot. Leave to stand for 3 minutes before serving.

Preheat the oven to 160°C fan (350°F), Gas Mark 4. Uncover the ovenproof container and then cover the top with foil. Place on a baking sheet in the centre of the oven for about 25–35 minutes or until piping hot. Leave to stand for 3 minutes before serving.

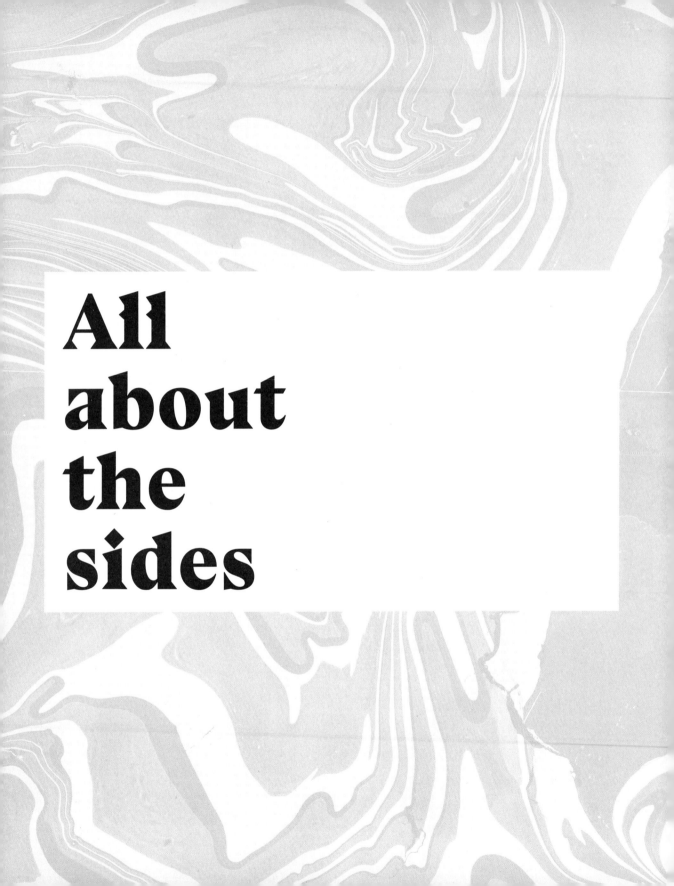

All about the sides

Super-easy rosemary & garlic roast potatoes

These roast potatoes are far superior to the shop-bought ones and so are well worth batch cooking. They certainly look impressive when served up on a busy weeknight. A stash of these in the freezer is a must in my house.

Makes 6–8 portions **DF / GF / V / VE**

150ml (5fl oz) vegetable oil
1kg (2lb 4oz) peeled and rinsed roasting potatoes, such as Maris Piper, patted dry, quartered or cut into even-sized chunks
5 garlic cloves, finely chopped
15g (½oz) rosemary, leaves picked and roughly chopped
1 tablespoon salt

1 Preheat the oven to 190°C fan (410°F), Gas Mark 6½.

2 Heat the vegetable oil in a roasting tray in the oven for 5 minutes.

3 Put the potatoes into a large bowl, add all the remaining ingredients and shake the bowl until the potatoes are coated with the garlic, rosemary and salt.

4 Carefully add the potatoes to the hot oil, making sure there is plenty of space around them, and roast for 45 minutes–1 hour, or until golden brown and cooked through.

5 Remove the potatoes from the oil, transfer briefly to a plate lined with kitchen paper to soak up any excess, and serve.

Portion out the roast potatoes into freezer-safe and ovenproof containers or dishes (see pages 8–9), making sure there is plenty of space around them and they are not squashed together. Leave to cool, then put the lids on or wrap tightly in clingfilm or foil, label and date (see page 9) before freezing.

Preheat the oven to 160°C fan (350°F), Gas Mark 4. Uncover the ovenproof container or dish and place on a baking sheet in the centre of the oven for 30–35 minutes or until piping hot. Leave to stand for 3 minutes before serving.

Indian turmeric potatoes
with spinach & mustard seeds

Packed with flavour, this makes a very impressive side dish to any curry. I have also enjoyed it on its own with a good dollop of coconut yogurt, chutney and Naan Breads (see page 148). Keep on standby in the freezer ready to enhance a curry feast night.

Makes 8–10 portions **DF / GF / V / VE**

1kg (2lb 4oz) new potatoes, quartered
vegetable oil
1 large onion, finely chopped
2cm (¾-inch) piece of fresh root ginger,
    peeled and finely chopped
3 garlic cloves, finely chopped
1 tablespoon ground turmeric
½ tablespoon ground cumin
1 tablespoon black mustard seeds
2 tablespoons water
400g (14oz) baby spinach leaves
15g (½oz) fresh coriander, roughly
    chopped (optional)
salt

1 Cook the potatoes in a large pan of boiling water for about 10 minutes, depending on their size, until just cooked through, then drain.

2 Meanwhile, heat a frying pan over a medium heat. Add a glug of vegetable oil and then the onion with a good pinch of salt and sweat for about 5 minutes until translucent.

3 Add the ginger and garlic and cook for a further 5 minutes.

4 Stir in the spices and cook for a minute. Then add the cooked potatoes and the measured water and stir until the potatoes are coated in the spices.

5 Add the spinach and cook for 3 minutes or until just wilted, then stir through the coriander, if using, and season to taste with salt.

Portion out the potato mixture into appropriate containers (see pages 8–9). Leave to cool, then seal, label and date (see page 9) before freezing.

 Microwave on high for 3 minutes, then remove from the microwave and uncover. Re-cover but don't seal and microwave for a further 5 minutes or until piping hot. Leave to stand for 3 minutes before serving.

Preheat the oven to 160°C fan (350°F), Gas Mark 4. Uncover the ovenproof container and then cover the top with foil. Place on a baking sheet in the centre of the oven for about 30–35 minutes or until piping hot. Leave to stand for 3 minutes before serving.

Dauphinoise potatoes

This classic recipe is a great one to master, to accompany any kind of casserole or pie for a truly comforting feast. It's the perfect make-ahead side and where freezing really comes into its own. After having a stash of these ready to go in the freezer, you'll never look back!

Makes 6–8 portions **GF**

20g (¾oz) unsalted butter
vegetable oil
1 large onion, thinly sliced
3 thyme sprigs, leaves picked and
   roughly chopped
3 garlic cloves, crushed
1kg (2lb 4oz) peeled and rinsed large
   potatoes, patted dry and thinly sliced,
   using a mandolin if you have one
1 litre (1¾ pints) double cream
400ml (14fl oz) milk
100g (3½oz) Parmesan cheese,
   finely grated
½ teaspoon freshly grated nutmeg
salt and pepper

1 Preheat the oven to 180°C fan (400°F), Gas Mark 6.

2 Heat a large, wide pan over a low heat. Melt the butter with a little vegetable oil, add the onion and sweat for 10–15 minutes until soft and translucent. Make sure you take your time with the onion, as this makes the dish so much tastier.

3 Add the thyme and garlic and cook for 5 minutes.

4 Stir in the potato slices, then remove the pan from the heat, pour in the cream and milk and add the Parmesan and nutmeg. Season generously with salt and pepper.

5 Lift out and layer the potato slices in a large baking dish, finishing just below the rim of the dish. Pour over the remaining cream mixture in the pan.

6 Bake for 40–45 minutes or until golden brown on top and the potato slices are cooked through.

 Portion out the dauphinoise mixture into freezer-safe and ovenproof containers or dishes (see pages 8–9). Leave to cool, then put the lids on or wrap tightly in clingfilm or foil, label and date (see page 9) before freezing.

Preheat the oven to 160°C fan (350°F), Gas Mark 4. Uncover the ovenproof container or dish and place on a baking sheet in the centre of the oven for 40–45 minutes or until piping hot. Leave to stand for 3 minutes before serving.

Carrot & parsnip purée

The great thing about puréeing vegetables is that you can use any ones you like and preferably ones that are in season, and it's the ideal way to use up vegetables that are getting a bit past their best. This is a real winter warmer and brings a little joy to any main meal, so it's well worth having to hand in the freezer. It's also very quick to make.

Makes 8–10 portions **GF / VE**

500g (1lb 2oz) carrots, peeled and diced
500g (1lb 2oz) parsnips, peeled and diced
50g (1¾oz) unsalted butter, cubed
15g (½oz) flat leaf parsley, leaves picked
  and roughly chopped
salt and pepper

1 Put the vegetables into a large pan, cover with water and bring to the boil. Then reduce the heat and simmer for about 20–25 minutes until cooked through.

2 Remove from the heat and drain, reserving some of the cooking liquid.

3 Blitz the cooked vegetables in a food processor or blender, gradually adding the butter as the machine is running, until you have a smooth purée. Add some of the reserved cooking liquid while blending to loosen the consistency if the purée is too thick.

4 Stir through the parsley and season to taste.

Portion out the vegetable purée into appropriate containers (see pages 8–9). Leave to cool, then seal, label and date (see page 9) before freezing.

Microwave on high for 3 minutes, then remove from the microwave and stir. Re-cover but don't seal and microwave for a further 5 minutes or until piping hot. Leave to stand for 3 minutes before serving.

Preheat the oven to 160°C fan (350°F), Gas Mark 4. Uncover the ovenproof container and then cover the top with foil. Place on a baking sheet in the centre of the oven for about 30–35 minutes or until piping hot. Leave to stand for 3 minutes before serving.

Roasted seasonal roots with herbs

I always seem to have vegetable leftovers in my vegetable box and this is my fail-safe way of making sure nothing is ever wasted. Swap any vegetable listed below to what you have or what's in season. This is such a versatile dish that will complement a wide variety of mains. Try serving it with some of our Best-ever Pesto (see page 140) for an extra-special salad or side.

Makes 8 portions **DF / GF / V / VE**

2 butternut squashes, peeled, deseeded and cut into wedges

5 large carrots, cut into 2–3cm (¾–1¼-inch) chunks

2 large red peppers, cored, deseeded and cut into 2–3cm (¾–1¼-inch) chunks

2 large yellow peppers, cored, deseeded and cut into 2–3cm (¾–1¼-inch) chunks

4 potatoes, peeled and cut into wedges

15g (½oz) sage

5 thyme sprigs

3 garlic cloves, crushed

3 tablespoons olive oil

15g (½oz) flat leaf parsley, leaves picked and roughly chopped

salt and pepper

1 Preheat the oven to 180°C fan (400°F), Gas Mark 6.

2 Put all the vegetables into a large bowl, add all the remaining ingredients except the parsley and season with salt and pepper. Mix until the ingredients are well combined.

3 Spread out on a large baking tray, making sure there is space between the vegetables, and roast for 35–40 minutes or until cooked through and starting to caramelize.

4 Mix the parsley through, adjust the seasoning and serve.

Portion out the roasted root mixture into appropriate containers (see pages 8–9). Leave to cool, then seal, label and date (see page 9) before freezing.

Microwave on high for 3 minutes, then remove from the microwave and stir. Re-cover but don't seal and microwave for a further 5 minutes or until piping hot. Leave to stand for 3 minutes before serving.

Preheat the oven to 160°C fan (350°F), Gas Mark 4. Uncover the ovenproof container and then cover the top with foil. Place on a baking sheet in the centre of the oven for about 40–45 minutes or until piping hot. Leave to stand for 3 minutes before serving.

Foolproof ratatouille

Equally good as a side or served with pasta or rice, this recipe is a crowd-pleaser and a fantastic way to get lots of different vegetables into one dish. It's great to have in the freezer ready to make a main meal extra special.

Makes 8-10 portions **DF / GF / V / VE**

vegetable oil
2 onions, finely chopped
4 garlic cloves, finely chopped
4 thyme sprigs, leaves picked and
   finely chopped
2 × 400g (14oz) cans chopped tomatoes
2 red onions, roughly chopped
2 courgettes, roughly chopped
2 red peppers, cored, deseeded and
   roughly chopped
2 yellow peppers, cored, deseeded and
   roughly chopped
50ml (2fl oz) olive oil
30g (1oz) basil, leaves picked and
   roughly chopped
15g (½oz) flat leaf parsley, leaves picked
   and chopped
grated zest and juice of 1 lemon
50ml (2fl oz) balsamic vinegar
salt and pepper

1 Heat a large, heavy-based pan over a medium heat. Add a good glug of vegetable oil and then the finely chopped onions and sweat for about 5–10 minutes until soft and translucent. Then add the garlic and thyme and cook for a minute.

2 Pour in the tomatoes and bring to a simmer. Then reduce the heat and simmer gently for about 30–35 minutes, stirring occasionally, until the sauce has thickened.

3 Meanwhile, preheat the oven to 180°C fan (400°F), Gas Mark 6.

Spread all the roughly chopped vegetables out on a large baking tray, season with salt and drizzle with the olive oil. Roast for 15–20 minutes or until tender and slightly caramelized.

4 Remove the tomato sauce from the heat and add the roasted vegetables. Stir in the remaining ingredients and season to taste.

Portion out the ratatouille mixture into appropriate containers (see pages 8–9). Leave to cool, then seal, label and date (see page 9) before freezing.

Microwave on high for 3 minutes, then remove from the microwave and stir. Re-cover but don't seal and microwave for a further 5 minutes or until piping hot. Leave to stand for 3 minutes before serving.

Preheat the oven to 160°C fan (350°F), Gas Mark 4. Uncover the ovenproof container and then cover the top with foil. Place on a baking sheet in the centre of the oven for about 30–35 minutes or until piping hot. Leave to stand for 3 minutes before serving.

Cauliflower & broccoli cheese

This comforting side dish is a family favourite and works well with many mains, so keep a stock in your freezer ready to serve at any given time. If you have made Ruby's Herb Crumb (see page 151), try sprinkling a handful on top before baking or freezing to add a next-level crunchy top.

Makes 8 portions

2 heads of cauliflower, florets and stalks cut into 2cm (¾-inch) chunks
2 heads of broccoli, florets and stalks cut into 2cm (¾-inch) chunks
50g (1¾oz) unsalted butter
50g (1¾oz) plain flour
500ml (18fl oz) milk
100g (3½oz) cheese of your choice, such as Cheddar, grated or crumbled
½ tablespoon Dijon mustard
1 teaspoon freshly grated nutmeg
50g (1¾oz) Parmesan cheese, finely grated
salt and pepper

1 If eating now, preheat the oven to 180°C fan (400°F), Gas Mark 6.

2 Cook the cauliflower and broccoli in a large pan of boiling water for about 5 minutes until just starting to soften – be careful not to overcook the vegetables at this stage, as they will turn mushy very quickly. Drain and set aside.

3 Melt the butter in a saucepan over a low heat, stir in the flour until the mixture forms a roux and cook for about 5 minutes, stirring constantly. Then gradually add the milk, whisking constantly until it is all incorporated and the sauce is smooth and thick.

4 Remove from the heat, stir in all the remaining ingredients except the Parmesan and season to taste.

5 Stir the cauliflower and broccoli through the sauce.

6 If you are eating now, transfer the cauliflower and broccoli mixture to a baking dish and sprinkle over the Parmesan. Bake for 20–25 minutes or until golden brown on top.

Portion out the cauliflower and broccoli mixture into appropriate containers (see pages 8–9), then sprinkle over an equal quantity of the Parmesan. Leave to cool, then seal, label and date (see page 9) before freezing.

Microwave on high for 3 minutes, then remove from the microwave and stir. Re-cover but don't seal and microwave for a further 5 minutes or until piping hot. Leave to stand for 3 minutes before serving.

Preheat the oven to 160°C fan (350°F), Gas Mark 4. Uncover the ovenproof container and place on a baking sheet in the centre of the oven for about 30–35 minutes or until golden brown on top and piping hot. Leave to stand for 3 minutes before serving.

Brilliant Brussels sprout gratin
with bacon & brandy

This is one of my best-loved recipes and it isn't just for Christmas! This superstar of a side dish is fantastic with any roast – give it a try and you will keep coming back for more. So I would advise keeping a good stock of it safely stowed in the freezer for those wintry days when you need a treat.

Makes 6–8 portions

1 large Savoy cabbage, cut into wedges
400g (14oz) Brussels sprouts, quartered
100g (3½oz) smoked lardons or streaky
  bacon, diced
2 garlic cloves, finely chopped
4 thyme sprigs, leaves picked
2 tablespoons olive oil
75g (2¾oz) unsalted butter
75g (2¾oz) plain flour
150ml (5fl oz) brandy
600ml (20fl oz) milk
300ml (10fl oz) double cream
1 teaspoon freshly grated nutmeg
60g (2¼oz) fresh white breadcrumbs
60g (2¼oz) Parmesan cheese, finely grated
salt and pepper
15g (½oz) flat leaf parsley, leaves picked
  and chopped, to garnish (optional)

1 Preheat the oven to 180°C fan (400°F), Gas Mark 6.

2 Toss the cabbage and sprouts with the lardons or bacon, garlic, thyme and olive oil on a large baking dish or roasting tin. Spread out, season with salt and pepper and roast for 15 minutes or until just cooked through and starting to caramelize.

3 Meanwhile, melt the butter in a saucepan over a low heat, stir in the flour until the mixture forms a roux and cook for about 5 minutes, stirring constantly. Then gradually add the brandy, whisking constantly, and cook for 2 minutes. Next, gradually add the milk, a little at a time, whisking constantly until it is all incorporated and the sauce is smooth and thick. Then whisk in the cream.

4 Remove from the heat and season with the nutmeg and salt and pepper to taste.

5 Pour the sauce over the roasted cabbage and sprouts on the baking dish or roasting tin, then sprinkle with the breadcrumbs and Parmesan.

6 If eating now, preheat the grill to medium–high (200°C/400°F).

7 Place under the hot grill and cook for 10 minutes or until golden brown and crispy on top. Leave to stand for 5 minutes before serving, garnished with the parsley, if you like.

Portion out the vegetable mixture into freezer-safe and ovenproof containers or dishes (see pages 8–9). Leave to cool, then put the lids on or wrap tightly in clingfilm or foil, label and date (see page 9) before freezing.

Preheat the oven to 160°C fan (350°F), Gas Mark 4. Uncover the ovenproof container or dish and place on a baking sheet in the centre of the oven for 40–45 minutes or until golden brown on top and piping hot. Leave to stand for 3 minutes before serving.

Mixed greens – leeks, peas & spinach

This is an invaluable dish to have under your belt – a side that will go with almost anything and a good way to get your greens in. I find myself reaching for this in the freezer almost every week.

Makes 8–10 portions **GF / VE**

vegetable oil
1 large onion, diced
4 large leeks, trimmed, cleaned and sliced
400g (14oz) frozen peas
300g (10½oz) frozen spinach or 400g (14oz) fresh spinach
200ml (7fl oz) double cream
grated zest and juice of 1 lemon
1 teaspoon freshly grated nutmeg
15g (½oz) flat leaf parsley, leaves picked and chopped
salt and pepper

1 Heat a large pan over a medium heat. Add a good glug of vegetable oil and then the onion with 1 teaspoon of salt and sweat for about 5 minutes until translucent.

2 Add the leeks and cook for about 5 minutes until they start to soften.

3 Then add the peas and spinach and cook for 5 minutes.

4 Stir in all the remaining ingredients and heat through, then season to taste.

❄️ Portion out the vegetable mixture into appropriate containers (see pages 8–9). Leave to cool, then seal, label and date (see page 9) before freezing.

🖼️ Microwave on high for 3 minutes, then remove from the microwave and stir. Re-cover but don't seal and microwave for a further 5 minutes or until piping hot. Leave to stand for 3 minutes before serving.

🍳 Preheat the oven to 160°C fan (350°F), Gas Mark 4. Uncover the ovenproof container and then cover the top with foil. Place on a baking sheet in the centre of the oven for about 30–35 minutes or until piping hot. Leave to stand for 3 minutes before serving.

Ruby's super grains

This is a great gluten-free wholegrain side dish that is really handy to have in the freezer as a healthier option to some other accompaniments. Easy to make in a large batch, it's perfect to bring out for a lunch or dinner on a busy day.

Makes 8 portions **DF / GF / V / VE**

400g (14oz) long-grain brown rice, well rinsed and drained
400g (14oz) dried Puy lentils, well rinsed and drained
400g (14oz) quinoa, well rinsed and drained
1 tablespoon olive oil
grated zest and juice of ½ lemon
30g (1oz) flat leaf parsley, leaves picked and chopped
salt and pepper

1 Put the rice into a pan with a lid and cover with water. Put the lid on the pan and bring to the boil. Reduce the heat and simmer for 25–30 minutes or until just cooked through, then drain.

2 Meanwhile, cook the lentils in a separate pan in the same way but without the lid and simmering for 30 minutes or until just cooked through, then drain.

3 At the same time, cook the quinoa in another pan in the same way as the lentils, for 20 minutes or until just cooked through, then drain.

4 Mix all the cooked grains together in a large bowl, then stir through all the remaining ingredients and season to taste.

Portion out the grain mixture into appropriate containers (see pages 8–9). Leave to cool, then seal, label and date (see page 9) before freezing.

Microwave on high for 3 minutes, then remove from the microwave and stir. Re-cover but don't seal and microwave for a further 5 minutes or until piping hot. Leave to stand for 3 minutes before serving.

Preheat the oven to 160°C fan (350°F), Gas Mark 4. Uncover the ovenproof container and then cover the top with foil. Place on a baking sheet in the centre of the oven for about 30–35 minutes or until piping hot. Leave to stand for 3 minutes before serving.

Fail-safe mixed rice with parsley

This rice dish has a great texture and visual appeal thanks to the addition of wild rice or black rice, with the parsley brightening the flavour. It's easy to make in a big batch for the freezer, ready to serve with many a main dish.

Makes 8–10 portions **DF** / **GF** / **V** / **VE**

200g (7oz) wild rice or black rice, well rinsed and drained
500g (1lb 2oz) basmati rice, well rinsed and drained
1 litre (1¾ pints) water
1 teaspoon salt
1 tablespoon chopped flat leaf parsley leaves

1 Put the wild rice or black rice into a pan, cover with plenty of water and bring to the boil. Reduce the heat and simmer, uncovered, for about 45–55 minutes for wild rice or 20 minutes for black rice or until just cooked through, then drain.

2 Meanwhile, put the basmati rice into a separate medium-sized pan and pour over the measured water. Put the lid on the pan and bring to the boil, then reduce the heat and simmer for 8 minutes, without lifting the lid. Turn the heat off, remove the lid and set aside, without stirring, for 10 minutes.

3 Mix the two cooked rices together, then stir through the salt and flat leaf parsley.

Portion out the rice mixture into appropriate containers (see pages 8–9). Leave to cool, then seal, label and date (see page 9) before freezing.

Microwave on high for 3 minutes, then remove from the microwave and stir. Re-cover but don't seal and microwave for a further 3 minutes or until piping hot. Leave to stand for 3 minutes before serving.

Preheat the oven to 160°C fan (350°F), Gas Mark 4. Uncover the ovenproof container and then cover the top with foil. Place on a baking sheet in the centre of the oven for about 30–35 minutes or until piping hot. Leave to stand for 3 minutes before serving.

The essentials

Super-duper tomato sauce

This tomato sauce is one that everyone loves in my household. Stuffed full of vegetables, it's ultra versatile – I use it on pizzas, to serve with pasta and as a sauce for chicken or fish. I always make a really big batch so that I have plenty in my freezer at all times. When stirring into pasta, I sometimes add a little cream cheese to make it a bit richer, which my children love!

Makes 6 adult-sized portions **DF / GF / V / VE**

olive oil
1 large onion, diced
1 garlic clove, crushed
1 celery stick, finely diced
½ teaspoon dried mixed herbs
250g (9oz) sweet potatoes, peeled and coarsely grated
250g (9oz) courgettes, coarsely grated
250g (9oz) carrots, coarsely grated
1 aubergine, diced
2 red peppers, cored, deseeded and diced
2 × 400g (14oz) cans chopped tomatoes
salt and pepper

1 Heat a large, heavy-based pan over a low heat. Add a good glug of olive oil and then the onion, garlic and celery with the dried mixed herbs and sweat for about 5 minutes until translucent.

2 Add the sweet potatoes, courgettes, carrots, aubergine and peppers and cook for about 15 minutes until softened.

3 Pour in the tomatoes, turn the heat up and bring to a simmer. Then reduce the heat and simmer gently for about 45 minutes, stirring occasionally.

4 Remove from the heat and leave to cool a little, then blitz with a hand blender or in a food processor or blender until smooth.

5 Season to taste.

Portion out the sauce into appropriate containers or freezer bags (see pages 8–9). Leave to cool, then seal, label and date (see page 9) before freezing.

Microwave on high for 3 minutes, then remove from the microwave and stir. Re-cover but don't seal and microwave for a further 3 minutes or until piping hot. Leave to stand for 3 minutes before serving.

Put the container or freezer bag into a bowl of hot water and leave for a few minutes until the contents are loosened from the container or bag sides. Transfer the contents to a pan and heat over a low heat until piping hot.

Best-ever pesto

This sauce is so useful to have frozen into a large silicone ice-cube tray or in small containers ready to pop out and add an explosion of flavour whenever you need. Try using some of this pesto mixed through roasted vegetables, as a delicious salad dressing or as a chicken marinade, besides in the more traditional way to brighten up any pasta dish. You can use the basic recipe as it stands or add different flavours to switch up your pesto stash.

Makes about 4 × 30g (1oz) tubs
GF / V and **VE** (if made with nutritional yeast flakes)

For basic pesto:
60g (2¼oz) basil, roughly chopped
3 tablespoons pine nuts, cashew nuts or blanched almonds, toasted
50g (1¾oz) Parmesan cheese, finely grated, or 2 tablespoons nutritional yeast flakes
1 teaspoon crushed garlic
2 tablespoons vegetable oil
4 teaspoons olive oil
juice of 1 lemon, or more if needed
salt

1 Put all the basic pesto ingredients except the salt into a food processor and blitz to your desired consistency. Alternatively, use a hand blender or a pestle and mortar.

2 Season to taste with salt and add more lemon juice if needed.

Variations:
For red pepper pesto:
2 roasted red peppers, skinned, deseeded and roughly chopped

For sun-dried tomato pesto:
5 sun-dried tomatoes in oil, drained

For spring herb pesto:
15g (½oz) mint, leaves picked and roughly chopped
15g (½oz) flat leaf parsley, leaves picked and roughly chopped

For harissa pesto:
1 tablespoon harissa

For spring greens pesto:
handful of baby spinach leaves, roughly chopped
20g (¾oz) cooked green beans, roughly chopped

To flavour your pesto with any of the suggested variations, simply blitz the ingredients along with those for the basic pesto.

Portion out the pesto into large ice-cube trays, freezer bags or individual small containers (see pages 8–9). Seal, label and date (see page 9) before freezing. If freezing in ice-cube trays, the frozen cubes can then be popped out directly into labelled freezer bags.

Add directly from frozen to hot pasta to melt, then heat through in the same pan as the pasta until hot.

If you are using the pesto as a dressing or marinade, put the freezer bag or container into a bowl of hot water and leave for a few minutes until the contents are defrosted. Alternatively, defrost at room temperature for about 1–2 hours before serving.

Salsa verde

This versatile sauce will add an explosion of flavour to all manner of dishes – use it as a dressing poured over salad leaves or roasted vegetables, add it to roast chicken or beef for instant gratification or enjoy in its classic pairing with lamb (see page 69). You can use any combination of herbs here depending on what's available.

Makes 8-10 portions **DF / GF**

6 salted anchovy fillets
2 garlic cloves, roughly chopped
3 oregano sprigs, leaves picked (optional)
15g (½oz) basil, leaves picked and
    roughly chopped
15g (½oz) mint, leaves picked and
    roughly chopped
15g (½oz) flat leaf parsley, leaves picked
    and roughly chopped
½ tablespoon Dijon mustard, or more
    to taste
1 tablespoon capers
3 tablespoons olive oil, or more if needed
1 tablespoon white wine vinegar, or more
    to taste
salt, if needed

1 Put all the ingredients into a food processor and blitz until combined but still chunky, adding a little more oil to loosen the consistency if needed. Alternatively, use a hand blender or a pestle and mortar.

2 Taste and adjust the mustard, vinegar and salt ratio to your personal preference.

Portion out the salsa verde into ice-cube trays, freezer bags or individual small containers (see pages 8–9). Seal, label and date (see page 9) before freezing. If freezing in ice-cube trays, the frozen cubes can then be popped out directly into labelled freezer bags.

If you are using the salsa verde as a dressing or marinade, put the freezer bag or container into a bowl of hot water and leave for a few minutes until the contents are defrosted. Alternatively, defrost at room temperature for about 1–2 hours before serving.

Chimichurri

My sister used to live in Argentina and I have very happy memories of eating chimichurri with steak, chips and salad. It's great with any grilled meat, fish, halloumi cheese or vegetables – perfect for a barbecue.

Makes 4–6 portions **DF / GF**

3 canned anchovy fillets
2 garlic cloves, crushed
½ teaspoon chilli flakes
1 teaspoon ground cumin
grated zest of 1 lemon
2 tablespoons red wine vinegar
50g (1¾oz) mixed herbs, such as flat leaf parsley, mint, fresh coriander and/or tarragon, any woody stalks discarded, roughly chopped
200ml (7fl oz) olive oil
salt and pepper

1 Put all the ingredients except the herbs, oil and seasoning into a food processor and blitz until smooth.

2 Add the herbs and blitz again until well blended. With the processor running, gradually pour in the olive oil until you have a loose consistency. Season to taste.

Freeze the chimichurri in large ice-cube trays or individual small containers (see pages 8–9). Seal, label and date (see page 9) before freezing. If freezing in ice-cube trays, the frozen cubes can then be popped out directly into labelled freezer bags.

Defrost the sauce at room temperature for about 1–2 hours before serving.

Classic vinaigrette

This silky smooth, super-easy vinaigrette is an absolute essential for quickly dressing a salad or drizzling over steamed green vegetables as an accompaniment to any of our main courses. It is the only recipe in the book that doesn't require freezing, as it will keep in the refrigerator for up to about 3 months.

Makes one 350ml (12fl oz) jar
DF / GF / VE

2 teaspoons clear honey
1 heaped teaspoon Dijon mustard
½ garlic clove, crushed
100ml (3½fl oz) sherry vinegar or
　cider vinegar
200ml (7fl oz) vegetable oil
salt and pepper

1 Put the honey, mustard and garlic into a thoroughly clean 350ml (12fl oz) airtight jar and stir together. Then whisk in the vinegar, followed by the vegetable oil.

2 Seal the jar with the lid and shake vigorously until well blended.

3 Store in the refrigerator, then shake the jar again before using, seasoning to taste.

Fast & flaky pastry

This is a fabulously easy and light flaky pastry, perfect for topping any pie. My stepmother always keeps a batch of this in the freezer, as it's a fail-safe staple.

Makes about 550g (1lb 4oz) pastry **VE**

225g (8oz) strong white flour, plus extra
　for dusting
175g (6oz) hard margarine, frozen for
　1 hour
150ml (5fl oz) ice-cold water

1 Put the flour into a large bowl and coarsely grate in the margarine. Stir in just enough of the measured ice-cold water with a round-bladed knife for the mixture to start coming together, then use your hands to form it into a dough.

2 Roll the dough out on a lightly floured work surface into a rectangle around 15cm (6 inches) wide and 1cm (½ inch) thick.

3 Fold in the short edges of the dough to meet in the centre and then fold in half. Give a quarter turn to the left, roll out again as before and repeat the folding process.

4 Wrap tightly in clingfilm or foil and refrigerate for at least 30 minutes before rolling out and using as instructed in your chosen recipe.

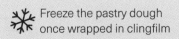 Freeze the pastry dough once wrapped in clingfilm or foil. Label and date (see page 9) before freezing.

 Defrost in the refrigerator for 24 hours before using.

Flatbreads

These are a game changer – so easy to make and a hundred times better than the supermarket equivalent. I always have some in the freezer. They are perfect with Ruby's One-pot Bean Chilli (see page 19) for a fajita night, or served with some dips to accompany pre-dinner drinks.

Makes 8 flatbreads **DF / V / VE**

250g (9oz) white or wholemeal plain flour, plus extra for dusting
1 teaspoon salt
150ml (5fl oz) water

1 Put the flour and salt into a large bowl and mix together. Then pour in the measured water and mix in initially with a wooden spoon and then bring the mixture together with your hands to form a dough.

2 Knead the dough on a lightly floured work surface for a few minutes until smooth.

3 Return the dough to the bowl, cover with a tea towel and leave to rest for about 30 minutes.

4 Divide the dough into eight balls and roll each one out on a lightly floured work surface as thinly as you can – about 2–3mm (1/16–1/8th inch) thick.

5 Heat a large, nonstick frying pan over a very high heat. Add one flatbread to the pan at a time and cook for about 30 seconds on each side until puffed up with a few patches of brown.

6 Remove the flatbread to a clean tea towel and wrap up to keep warm and soft until ready to serve.

You can freeze either the rested dough (after step 3) or the cooked, cooled flatbreads. Wrap the dough or flatbreads tightly in clingfilm or foil or put into freezer bags. Seal, label and date (see page 9) before freezing.

Unwrap the frozen flatbreads, place them in a stack on a microwave-safe plate, cover in clingfilm and microwave on high for 1–2 minutes. Leave to stand for about 30 seconds before serving.

Preheat the oven to 160°C fan (350°F), Gas Mark 4. Wrap the frozen flatbreads in foil and heat for 10 minutes or until warmed through.

Defrost the dough in the refrigerator for about 24 hours, then follow steps 4–6 above to prepare and cook the flatbreads.

Naan breads

These delicious homemade naan breads are great served with any of our curries and are such a useful item to have in the freezer. Whether as uncooked dough or cooked breads, this recipe freezes really well.

Makes 6 naan breads **VE**

250g (9oz) strong white flour, plus extra
    for dusting
½ tablespoon coarse sea salt
1 tablespoon nigella seeds
7g sachet (2¼ teaspoons) fast-action
    dried yeast
45g (1½oz) unsalted butter
3 tablespoons full-fat natural yogurt
1 teaspoon clear honey

1 Put the flour, salt, nigella seeds and yeast in a large bowl and mix together.

2 Melt 15g (½oz) of the butter in a small pan over a low heat. Pour the melted butter into a jug or small bowl, add the yogurt and honey and whisk together until combined.

3 Make a well in the centre of the dry ingredients and pour the wet ingredients into it. Mix in initially with a fork and then bring the mixture together with your hands to form a dough. The dough should be quite sticky and soft, so add a splash of water if necessary.

4 Knead the dough on a lightly floured work surface for about 5 minutes until smooth.

5 Return the dough to a lightly floured bowl, cover with a tea towel and leave to rise in a warm place for about 1½ hours until doubled in size.

6 Turn the dough out on to a floured work surface and knead firmly for a few minutes to knock out the excess air until smooth again.

7 Divide the dough into six balls and roll each one out into an oval about 1cm (½ inch) thick.

8 Heat a large, nonstick frying pan over a very high heat. Meanwhile, melt the remaining butter in a small pan over a low heat. Add one naan to the frying pan at a time and cook for about 2–3 minutes on each side until cooked through and lightly browned.

9 Remove the naan to a clean tea towel and brush both sides with the melted butter. Cover with another clean tea towel and keep warm until ready to serve.

You can freeze either the proved dough (after step 6) or the cooked, cooled naan breads. Wrap the dough or naan breads tightly in clingfilm or foil or put into freezer bags. Seal, label and date (see page 9) before freezing.

Unwrap the frozen naan breads, place them in a stack on a microwave-safe plate, uncovered, and microwave on high for 1–2 minutes. Leave to stand for 30 seconds before serving.

Preheat the oven to 160°C fan (350°F), Gas Mark 4. Unwrap the frozen naan breads, place on a baking sheet and heat for 5–10 minutes or until warmed through.

Defrost the dough in the refrigerator for about 24 hours, then follow steps 7–9 above to prepare and cook the naan breads.

Classic chicken broth

This soup will bring anyone feeling a little under the weather or in need of a pick-me-up some warming comfort, like a hug in a bowl. Deeply nourishing and energizing, this is definitely one to have stashed in the freezer on standby. You can also use this soup as a chicken stock, to make gravy or to add an injection of flavour.

Makes 8–10 portions **DF / GF**

1 medium chicken, about 1.5kg (3lb 5oz)
olive oil
2kg (4lb 8oz) raw or cooked chicken bones
2 tablespoons vegetable oil
3 onions, roughly chopped
6 carrots, roughly chopped
1 head of celery, roughly chopped
30g (1oz) flat leaf parsley, stalks only
3 fresh or dried bay leaves
10 black peppercorns
3 litres (5¼ pints) water
salt and pepper

1 Preheat the oven to 180°C fan (400°F), Gas Mark 6.

2 Place the chicken in a roasting tray, season with salt and pepper and drizzle with olive oil. Roast for about an hour or until the juices run clear when the thickest part of the thigh is pierced with a skewer and the internal temperature of the chicken reaches above 74°C (165°F) on a meat thermometer.

3 Meanwhile, spread the chicken bones out on a large baking tray and roast for 30 minutes or until golden brown.

4 Leave the chicken to cool, then pick the meat off the bones and shred it, reserving any bones but discarding the skin. Transfer the chicken to a plate, cover with clingfilm and place in the refrigerator.

5 Put all the roasted bones and chicken carcass into a large, heavy-based pan over a medium heat. Add the vegetable oil and then the vegetables and sweat for about 10 minutes until softened.

6 Add all the remaining ingredients and bring to the boil. Then reduce the heat and simmer for 2–3 hours, stirring occasionally and skimming off any excess fat.

7 Strain the stock through a strainer and discard the bones, vegetables and seasonings.

8 To serve, divide the roast chicken meat between bowls, then pour over the hot stock.

Portion out the chicken meat into appropriate containers (see pages 8–9). Leave the stock to cool, then pour an equal quantity over each portion. Seal, label and date (see page 9) before freezing.

 Microwave on high for 3 minutes, then remove from the microwave and stir. Re-cover but don't seal and microwave for a further 5 minutes or until piping hot. Leave to stand for 3 minutes before serving.

Put the container into a bowl of hot water and leave for a few minutes until the contents are loosened from the container sides. Transfer the contents to a pan and heat over a low heat until piping hot. Leave to stand for 3 minutes before serving.

Ruby's herb crumb

We developed a herb crumb at ByRuby to bring an extra texture and flavour dimension to many of our oven-cooked dishes. I highly recommend making this in a large batch so that you can try sprinkling it over our Best-ever Macaroni Cheese (see page 97), Vegetable Lasagne with Butternut Squash & Aubergine (see page 81), Ruby's Fabulous Fish Pie (see page 57) and Cauliflower & Broccoli Cheese (see page 128), among others, before baking. It also works really well sprinkled over any pasta dish before serving.

Makes 8 portions

½ loaf of white bread, about 400g (14oz), preferably slightly stale
15g (½oz) flat leaf parsley, leaves picked and roughly chopped
4 garlic cloves, finely chopped
grated zest of 2 lemons

1 Preheat the oven to 180°C fan (400°F), Gas Mark 6.

2 Cut the bread into small pieces, spread out on a baking sheet and toast for about 10 minutes, depending on how fresh the bread is, until dry and crisp.

3 Leave to cool, then transfer the bread to a food processor, add all the remaining ingredients and blitz to crumbs. If you don't have a food processor, finely chop the parsley and crush the garlic, then add to a bowl with the lemon zest and toasted bread. Crush the toasted bread into crumbs with the end of a rolling pin.

4 Whether using immediately or from the freezer, simply sprinkle the crumb on top of oven-cooked dishes before baking or over pasta dishes before serving.

Portion out the crumb mixture into freezer bags (see pages 8–9). Seal, label and date (see page 9) before freezing.

Flavour-packed butters

These butters are packed with flavour, they're super easy to make and will turn a midweek meal into a triumph. Having a set of these in the freezer ready to pull out at any time is a must. Try adding to meat hot off the barbecue so that it soaks up all the flavour while resting. Or place a slice on top of fish or insert under the skin of a chicken before roasting. You can also rub your cooked corn cobs into the butter or add a few slices to freshly made Flatbreads (see page 146). There are so many possibilities!

Makes one 250g (9oz) pack of butter, about 10 slices

250g (9oz) unsalted butter, softened

For sumac & za'atar butter:
1 tablespoon sumac
½ tablespoon za'atar
good pinch of salt

For dukkah butter:
50g (1¾oz) hazelnuts, roughly chopped
1 tablespoon cumin seeds, crushed
1 tablespoon fennel seeds, crushed
1 tablespoon coriander seeds, crushed
2 tablespoons sesame seeds, toasted
good pinch of salt

1 Put the softened butter into a bowl and add the ingredients for your chosen flavour, then beat together until well combined.

2 Arrange the mixture on a sheet of nonstick baking paper in a rough log shape along one side. Roll up in the paper into a neat log shape. If using now, chill in the freezer for 20–25 minutes or until firm.

❄ Wrap the paper-covered log of butter tightly in clingfilm or foil. Label and date (see page 9) before freezing. When ready to use, remove the butter from the freezer, unwrap and, using a sharp knife, cut off as many slices as you want. Use directly from frozen – the butter will take only a few minutes to soften up when placed directly on top of hot food. Rewrap the remaining butter as before and return to the freezer.

Sumac & za'atar butter

For harissa butter:
2 tablespoons harissa
grated zest and juice of 2 lemons
2 teaspoons dried mint
good pinch of salt

For lemon & garlic butter:
3 garlic cloves, crushed with the flat blade
   of a knife with a little salt to a paste
grated zest and juice of 2 lemons
2 teaspoons dried oregano

For lime & chilli butter:
1cm (½-inch) piece of fresh root ginger,
   peeled and grated
1 red chilli, deseeded and finely chopped
1 garlic clove, crushed with the flat blade
   of a knife with a little salt to a paste
grated zest and juice of 2 limes
15g (½oz) fresh coriander, leaves picked
   and roughly chopped (optional)
good pinch of salt

For herb butter:
1 garlic clove, crushed with the flat blade
   of a knife with a little salt to a paste
30g (1oz) flat leaf parsley, leaves picked
   and finely chopped
15g (½oz) tarragon, leaves picked and
   finely chopped
15g (½oz) thyme, leaves picked and
   finely chopped
(or use any herbs you have)
good pinch of salt

Sweet treats

Brilliant brownies

These are hands down the best brownies ever. I have made these countless times for friends, as birthday gifts or for a new mum. You can turn them into mega brownies by simply adding a topping of your choice halfway through baking – see my suggestions below. Keep a stash in your freezer to delight unexpected guests, or on standby for a special occasion or just for a midweek pick-me-up.

Makes 24 brownies **GF / VE**

5 large eggs
390g (13½oz) caster sugar
140g (5oz) cocoa powder
250g (9oz) coconut oil, melted
110g (3¾oz) ground almonds
2 teaspoons gluten-free baking powder
1 teaspoon salt

For the topping (optional):
250g (9oz) chopped mixed nuts
OR 3 tablespoons crunchy peanut butter
OR 250g (9oz) frozen or fresh raspberries

1 Preheat the oven to 160°C fan (350°F), Gas Mark 4. Line a traybake tin, about 30 × 23 × 4cm (12 × 9 × 1½ inches), with nonstick baking paper.

2 Put the eggs and sugar into a large bowl and beat together with an electric hand mixer or in a stand mixer until pale, thick and a ribbon of mixture falling from the whisk or mixer attachment when lifted from the mixture holds its shape. This usually takes a good 5–10 minutes using an electric hand mixer.

3 Sift the cocoa into the melted coconut oil, then beat into the egg mixture until combined.

4 Mix the ground almonds, baking powder and salt together, then fold into the egg mixture with a large metal spoon.

5 Pour the batter into the lined tin and bake for 10 minutes. If using a topping, remove the brownie from the oven and sprinkle or spread over your chosen topping before baking for a further 15–20 minutes or until cooked through but with a slight wobble in the middle.

6 Leave to cool completely in the tin, then cut into 24 portions to serve. The brownies will keep in an airtight container for up to 3–4 days or for up to 1 year in the freezer stored at -18°C (-0.4°F).

Put the individual cooled brownies into freezer-safe containers, and microwave-safe if wanting to defrost in the microwave (see pages 8–9). Seal, label and date (see page 9) before freezing.

Transfer the brownies to a microwave-safe plate and microwave on high, covered, for 1–2 minutes or until just soft.

 Defrost for 1–2 hours or until soft before serving.

Passionfruit tart

Rich and creamy, this is a sure-fire dessert for a dinner party. If making the pastry from scratch is a step too far, use ready-made shortcrust pastry. Serve with softly whipped cream sweetened with a little icing sugar and spiked with lime zest.

Makes one 24cm (9½-inch) tart, 6 portions **VE**

For the pastry:
250g (9oz) plain flour, plus extra for dusting
75g (2¾oz) icing sugar, plus extra for dusting
120g (4¼oz) unsalted butter, cut into cubes and chilled
3 egg yolks, beaten
2 tablespoons ice-cold water

For the passionfruit cream:
5 eggs
100g (3½oz) caster sugar
170ml (6fl oz) ready-made passionfruit purée
70ml (2½fl oz) double cream

1 For the pastry, put the flour and icing sugar into a bowl and mix together. Add the butter and rub in with your fingertips until the mixture resembles breadcrumbs. Alternatively, pulse the ingredients together in a food processor. Stir in the egg yolks and measured water with a round-bladed knife, then use your hands to bring the mixture together to form a dough. Alternatively, with the food processor running, gradually pour in the egg yolks and water until a dough forms.

2 Roll the dough out on a lightly floured work surface large enough to line a 24cm (9½-inch) round tart tin. Lay the pastry over the tin and press it gently into the corners and sides, using a bit of spare dough as it will be a little sticky, then patch up any holes with more spare dough. Freeze for about 15 minutes until firm.

3 Meanwhile, preheat the oven to 160°C fan (350°F), Gas Mark 4.

4 Line the pastry case with nonstick baking paper and fill with baking beans. Bake for 20–30 minutes until the sides are pale golden brown.

5 While the pastry case is baking, beat the eggs with the sugar in a large bowl until well combined, then stir in the passionfruit purée and cream. Pour the mixture into a pan and heat over a low heat, stirring constantly, until just a bit warmer than body temperature, about 40°C (104°F) on a food thermometer.

6 Remove the pastry case from the oven and lift out the paper and beans. Pour the passionfruit cream very carefully into the pastry case, being careful not to spill it over the edges, and bake for 10–15 minutes until the filling is just set but with a slight wobble in the middle. Leave to cool completely in the tin.

7 If serving now, remove the tart from the tin and dust with icing sugar. The cooled (or defrosted) tart can be kept in the refrigerator, covered with clingfilm, for up to 24 hours.

Wrap the tin with the cooled tart in it tightly in clingfilm or foil. Label and date (see page 9) before freezing.

Defrost in the refrigerator for 24 hours. Leave at room temperature for 2 hours before serving, dusted with icing sugar.

Chocolate chip cookies

This recipe comes from Finns, the wonderful food shop in Chelsea, South West London, where ByRuby originated. Keeping the dough ready to bake in the freezer means you're never more than 15 minutes away from enjoying these dangerously delicious cookies. And they keep well too once baked, although I've never known them hang around for long. I like to use a mixture of white and dark chocolate chips.

Makes 16-20 cookies **VE**

200g (7oz) unsalted butter, softened
200g (7oz) caster sugar
2 eggs, beaten
250g (9oz) plain flour, plus extra for dusting
½ teaspoon bicarbonate of soda
300g (10½oz) chocolate chips

1 Put the butter and sugar into a large bowl and beat together with an electric hand mixer or wooden spoon or in a stand mixer until pale and fluffy. Then beat in the eggs until incorporated.

2 Sift the flour and bicarbonate of soda together into the cookie mixture and mix in with a wooden spoon. Stir in the chocolate chips, then use your hands to bring the mixture together to form a dough.

3 Roll the dough on a lightly floured work surface into an even sausage shape around 4cm (1½ inches) in diameter. Wrap tightly in clingfilm or foil and freeze for at least 20 minutes.

4 If baking now, meanwhile, preheat the oven to 160°C fan (350°F), Gas Mark 4. Line a baking sheet with nonstick baking paper.

5 Remove the dough from the freezer, unwrap and, using a sharp knife, slice into rounds about 5mm (¼ inch) thick.

6 Lay the dough rounds, spaced apart, on the lined baking sheet and bake for 10 minutes until pale golden brown.

7 Transfer to a wire rack and leave to cool completely. The cookies will keep in an airtight container for up to a month.

Label and date (see page 9) the clingfilm- or foil-wrapped dough before freezing.

When ready to use, unwrap the frozen dough, then follow steps 4–7 above to slice, bake and cool the cookies.

Butter biscuits

Freshly baked biscuits will always be at your fingertips if you keep a log of this dough in your freezer. I always used to make these with my granny as a child, and they are a great way to get the kids involved in baking.

Makes 16 biscuits **VE**

100g (3½oz) unsalted or salted butter, softened
50g (1¾oz) caster sugar
150g (5½oz) self-raising flour, plus extra for dusting

1 Put the butter and sugar into a bowl and beat together with an electric hand mixer or a wooden spoon until well combined. Stir in the flour initially with a wooden spoon, then use your hands to bring the mixture together to form a dough.

2 Roll the dough on a lightly floured work surface into an even sausage shape about 2.5cm (1 inch) in diameter. Wrap tightly in clingfilm or foil and freeze for at least 15 minutes.

3 If baking now, meanwhile, preheat the oven to 180°C fan (400°F), Gas Mark 6. Line a baking sheet with nonstick baking paper.

4 Remove the dough from the freezer, unwrap and, using a sharp knife, slice into rounds about 5mm (¼ inch) thick.

5 Lay the dough rounds, spaced about 2cm (¾ inch) apart, on the lined baking sheet and prick each one with a fork a couple of times. Bake for 15–20 minutes until very pale golden brown.

6 Transfer to a wire rack and leave to cool completely. The biscuits will keep in an airtight container for up to a month.

Label and date (see page 9) the clingfilm- or foil-wrapped dough before freezing.

When ready to use, unwrap the frozen dough, then follow steps 3–6 above to slice, bake and cool the biscuits.

Ruby's super sticky toffee pudding

I always order sticky toffee pudding if it's on a menu, as it's my favourite. It's so comforting and delicious, especially served with a good dollop of ice cream. With a stock of this classic sweet treat in the freezer, you can't go wrong.

Makes 12 portions **VE**

For the sponge:
400g (14oz) pitted dates, roughly chopped
4 teaspoons bicarbonate of soda
400ml (14fl oz) boiling water
150g (5½oz) unsalted or salted butter, softened
250g (9oz) light soft brown sugar
4 eggs
400g (14oz) plain flour
2 teaspoons vanilla bean paste

For the sauce:
550g (1lb 4oz) light soft brown sugar
300g (10½oz) unsalted or salted butter
2 tablespoons black treacle
400ml (14fl oz) double cream

1 Preheat the oven to 180°C fan (400°F), Gas Mark 6. Place a paper case in each of the holes of a 12-hole silicone or tin muffin tray or line a 900g (2lb) loaf tin with nonstick baking paper.

2 For the sponge, put the dates, bicarbonate of soda and measured boiling water in a bowl and set aside.

3 Put the butter and sugar into a large bowl and beat together with an electric hand mixer or wooden spoon or in a stand mixer until pale and fluffy.

4 Add the eggs, one at a time, beating well after each addition and adding a little of the flour if the mixture looks like it is splitting.

5 Fold in the flour and vanilla with a large metal spoon.

6 Mash the dates with the back of a spoon to a paste-like consistency, then fold into the cake batter.

7 Pour the batter into the prepared cake tins until three-quarters full or into the loaf tin. Bake the individual cakes for about 25 minutes or the loaf for about 35 minutes until springy to the touch and a skewer inserted into the centre comes out clean.

8 Meanwhile, put all the sauce ingredients except the cream into a pan and heat over a medium heat, stirring constantly, until the sugar has dissolved. Then stir in the cream and remove from the heat.

9 Turn the cakes or loaf out on to a wire rack, peel off the lining paper from the loaf or the individual paper cases from the cakes and leave to cool slightly. If eating now, transfer the warm cakes, or the warm loaf cut into 12 slices, to serving dishes and pour over the warm sauce.

Put the individual cakes or slices into appropriate containers or the whole loaf into a large airtight container (see pages 8–9), then pour over the warm sauce. Leave to cool, then seal, label and date (see page 9) before freezing.

Microwave on high for 3 minutes, then remove from the microwave and uncover. Replace the lid but don't seal and microwave for a further 2 minutes or until piping hot. Leave to stand for 3 minutes before serving.

Preheat the oven to 160°C fan (350°F), Gas Mark 4. Uncover the ovenproof container and then cover the top with foil. Place on a baking sheet in the centre of the oven for 30–35 minutes or until piping hot. Leave to stand for 3 minutes before serving.

Gooey chocolate cake

This is an easy, versatile recipe that can be made into muffins, a round cake or a loaf. It's equally good as a sumptuous make-ahead dessert to serve warm or cold or as a birthday cake, decorated with raspberries and chopped nuts.

Makes about 12 muffins or 10-12 portions **VE**

For the cake:
vegetable oil, for greasing
225g (8oz) plain flour
1½ teaspoons bicarbonate of soda
½ teaspoon fine salt
1½ teaspoons instant coffee powder
75g (2¾oz) cocoa powder
300g (10½oz) dark soft brown sugar
375ml (13fl oz) hot water from the kettle, slightly cooled
75g (2¾oz) coconut oil
1½ teaspoons cider vinegar

For the icing:
40g (1½oz) cocoa powder
40g (1½oz) caster sugar
20g (¾oz) margarine
100ml (3½fl oz) oat milk, or more if you like

1 Preheat the oven to 180°C fan (400°F), Gas Mark 6.

2 Grease the holes of a 12-hole silicone or tin muffin tray with vegetable oil, or grease and line the base and sides of a 28cm (11-inch) springform cake tin or a 900g (2lb loaf tin) with nonstick baking paper.

3 Put the flour, bicarbonate of soda, salt, coffee powder and cocoa into a bowl and mix together.

4 In a separate bowl, mix the sugar, measured hot water, coconut oil and vinegar together until the coconut oil has melted. Then stir into the dry ingredients until well combined.

5 Divide the batter between the greased muffin tray holes or pour into the prepared cake or loaf tin. Bake the muffins for 20–25 minutes or the cake or loaf for 30–35 minutes until springy to the touch and a skewer inserted into the centre comes out clean.

6 Meanwhile, put all the icing ingredients into a heavy-based pan and bring to the boil, stirring until the sugar has dissolved. Whisk until the mixture looks glossy, adding a little more oat milk if you prefer a thinner consistency.

7 Turn the muffins out or release the cake or loaf on to a plate, peel off the lining paper from the cake or loaf then pour over the warm icing and serve while still warm (which is best) or leave to cool.

Leave the iced muffins or cake or loaf to cool completely. Put the muffins or slices of the cake or loaf into appropriate containers or individual ramekins, or the whole cake or loaf into a large airtight container (see pages 8–9). Seal or wrap the ramekins tightly in clingfilm or foil, label and date (see page 9, but in this case the best before date is 3 months) before freezing.

Microwave on high, covered, for 3 minutes. Leave to stand for 2 minutes before serving.

Preheat the oven to 160°C fan (350°F), Gas Mark 4. For muffins or cake slices, uncover the ovenproof container then cover with foil. Place on a baking sheet in the centre of the oven for 10–15 minutes until warmed through. For an entire cake, place on a baking sheet in the centre of the oven for 20 minutes until warmed through.

Defrost at room temperature for 2 hours or in the fridge for 1–4 hours to serve cold.

Eton mess semifreddo

A fantastic showstopper that won't fail to impress yet is easy to make, this is the perfect laid-back summer dessert that can be served straight from the freezer.

Makes about 10 portions **GF / VE**

400g (14oz) fresh mixed berries, such as raspberries and strawberries, plus extra to decorate
250g (9oz) icing sugar
grated zest and juice of 2 lemons
8 large egg whites
1 litre (1¾ pints) double cream
100g (3½oz) meringue nests, crumbled

1 Line a 900g (2lb) loaf tin with clingfilm and set aside.

2 Put the berries, 100g (3½oz) of the icing sugar and the lemon juice into a pan and heat gently for about 5 minutes until the berries have softened and the liquid is syrupy.

3 Using a slotted spoon, remove half the berries and reserve, then blitz the remainder with a hand blender or in a blender until smooth.

4 Push the berry purée through a fine sieve into a bowl, discarding any pips. Leave the purée and reserved berries to cool.

5 Whisk the egg whites in a large bowl with an electric hand mixer until stiff peaks form. Add the remaining icing sugar and beat again until the mixture is smooth, thick and glossy.

6 In a separate bowl, whip the cream until it holds its shape, being careful not to overwhip.

7 Using a large metal spoon, gently fold the whisked egg whites and lemon zest into the cream, then fold in the crumbled meringue.

8 Fold through the cooled berry purée and reserved whole berries.

9 Transfer the mixture to the prepared loaf tin. Freeze the dessert for at least 8 hours before serving.

10 To serve, turn out the semifreddo and cut into slices. Decorate with extra berries.

Wrap the loaf tin of semifreddo tightly in clingfilm or foil. Label and date (see page 9) before freezing.

Unwrap and serve straight away in slices or leave to sit at room temperature for about 10 minutes until slightly softened before serving.

Tiramisu

This classic dessert is such a crowd-pleaser and easy to make in big batches. I have pulled this out of the freezer for many a dinner party to nothing but praise from my guests.

Makes about 10–12 portions VE

1 litre (1¾ pints) double cream
500g (1lb 2oz) mascarpone cheese
150ml (5fl oz) Marsala wine
300g (10½oz) caster sugar
2 teaspoons vanilla bean paste
300g (10½oz) sponge fingers
100ml (3½fl oz) freshly brewed very
  strong espresso coffee, cooled to
  room temperature
50g (1¾oz) dark chocolate (at least
  70% cocoa solids)
1 tablespoon cocoa powder

1 Put the cream, mascarpone, Marsala wine, sugar and vanilla into a large bowl and beat together with an electric hand mixer or balloon whisk until thick and completely smooth, being careful not to overwhip the cream.

2 Soak the sponge fingers in the coffee for a few minutes each side, but no longer, otherwise they will go soggy.

3 Arrange half the sponge fingers in a layer in the base of a trifle dish or serving bowl, then add half the cream mixture and grate over about half the chocolate.

4 Repeat with the remaining sponge fingers and cream mixture.

5 Dust the top of the tiramisu with the cocoa powder and grate over the remaining chocolate.

6 If eating now, refrigerate for 3–4 hours until set, or overnight, before serving.

Wrap the dish or bowl of tiramisu tightly in clingfilm or foil. Label and date (see page 9) before freezing.

Defrost in the refrigerator for 12 hours or overnight until the mixture is soft to the touch before serving.

Peggy's gingerbread

This recipe comes from a wonderful lady called Peggy, who looked after Milly's husband Harry when he was a child. Her instruction was 'be heavy-handed with the treacle!' Sticky and spiced, the addition of wholemeal flour gives this a wonderful texture. Serve with ice cream as a dessert or at teatime with a cuppa.

Makes 16 generous slices **VE**

vegetable oil, for greasing
225g (8oz) white plain flour
225g (8oz) wholemeal plain flour
225g (8oz) hard margarine, cut into cubes
   and chilled
340g (11¾oz) caster sugar
2 tablespoons bicarbonate of soda
570ml (1 pint) boiling water
2 generous tablespoons golden syrup
2 generous tablespoons black treacle
2 tablespoons ground ginger
2 eggs, beaten

1 Preheat the oven to 160°C fan (350°F), Gas Mark 4. Grease a traybake tin, about 30 × 23 × 4cm (12 × 9 × 1½ inches), and line with nonstick baking paper.

2 Put the flours into a large bowl and mix together. Add the margarine and rub in with your fingertips until the mixture resembles breadcrumbs. Alternatively, pulse the ingredients together in a food processor. Mix in the sugar.

3 Stir the bicarbonate of soda into the measured boiling water in a jug, then add to the flour mixture with all the remaining ingredients, adding the eggs last.

4 Beat the ingredients together until smooth or blitz them together in the food processor.

5 Pour the batter (it will be very wet) into the lined tin and bake for 45–55 minutes until springy to the touch.

6 If eating now, leave to cool in the tin for a few minutes, then turn out on to a wire rack. If freezing, leave to cool completely in the tin. Slice and serve warm or cold. The gingerbread will keep in an airtight container for up to about a week.

Wrap the cooled gingerbread tightly in clingfilm or foil. If you want to serve warm from frozen, slice and freeze in portions of two slices wrapped in clingfilm (if reheating in the microwave) or foil (if reheating in the oven). Label and date (see page 9) before freezing.

Microwave on high wrapped in clingfilm for 1 minute. Leave to stand for 2 minutes before serving.

Preheat the oven to 160°C fan (350°F), Gas Mark 4. Heat wrapped in foil for 5–10 minutes until warmed through.

Defrost the whole tray in the refrigerator for 24 hours before serving.

Classic Victoria sponge

The Queen of Cakes, who doesn't love a Vicky sponge sandwiched together with luxuriously creamy buttercream and summer berry jam? What's more, you can freeze this in all its glory ready to serve in an upturned cake tin!

Makes one 23cm (9-inch) cake **VE**

4 tablespoons strawberry or raspberry jam
fresh berries, to decorate (optional)

For the sponge:
300g (10½oz) unsalted butter, softened, plus
    extra for greasing (or use vegetable oil)
300g (10½oz) caster sugar
4 eggs
300g (10½oz) plain flour
2 teaspoons baking powder
dash of milk

For the buttercream:
300g (10½oz) unsalted butter, softened
600g (1lb 5oz) icing sugar, sifted, plus extra
    (optional) for dusting

1 Preheat the oven to 160°C fan (350°F), Gas Mark 4. Grease two 23cm (9-inch) loose-bottomed sandwich cake tins and line the bases with nonstick baking paper.

2 Put all the sponge ingredients into a large bowl and beat together with an electric hand mixer or a wooden spoon or in a food processor or stand mixer until well combined and smooth.

3 Divide the batter between the prepared tins and spread level, then bake for 25–30 minutes or until golden, springy to the touch and a skewer inserted into the centre comes out clean. Leave the cakes to cool in the tins for 5 minutes, then turn out on to a wire rack, peel off the lining paper and leave to cool completely.

4 For the buttercream, beat the butter in a large bowl until soft, then gradually beat in the icing sugar until pale and fluffy, adding a dash of hot water if it's difficult to work.

5 When the cakes are cool, trim so that the top of each cake is level if necessary. Spread the jam over the top of the bottom cake and then spread half the buttercream on top. Cover with the other cake and spread the top with the remaining buttercream. The cake will keep in an airtight cake tin for up to about 3 days.

6 To serve, decorate the top of the cake with some fresh berries and add a dusting of icing sugar, if you like.

Stand the fully assembled cake on the lid of an airtight cake tin, then cover with the tin. Label and date (see page 9) before freezing.

Defrost at room temperature for 6–8 hours or in the refrigerator for 24 hours. Decorate as in step 6 above before serving.

Glossary of UK/US terms

UK	US
aubergine	eggplant
baking sheet	cookie sheet
baking tray	baking sheet
bicarbonate of soda	baking soda
black treacle	blackstrap molasses
caster sugar	superfine sugar
clingfilm	plastic wrap
coriander (fresh)	cilantro
courgette	zucchini
dark chocolate	bittersweet chocolate
desiccated coconut	dried unsweetened coconut
double cream	heavy cream
frying pan	skillet
golden syrup	light corn syrup
grill	broiler
hob	stovetop
icing	frosting
icing sugar	confectioners' sugar
kitchen paper	paper towels
knock back/out	punch down
minced beef/pork	ground beef/pork
pak choi	bok choy
passata	strained/sieved tomatoes
peppers (red, orange, yellow, green)	bell peppers
piping bag	pastry bag
plain flour	all-purpose flour
self-raising flour	self-rising flour
sieve	strainer
sponge fingers	ladyfingers
spring onions	scallions
stock cube	bouillon cube
tea towel	dish towel
tin	pan
tomato purée	tomato paste
wholemeal flour	whole wheat flour

Index

Acknowledgements

A huge thank you to our families. Our joint love for food and cooking began at home; without this, ByRuby would not be.

Thank you to all of our wonderful team at ByRuby for all of their hard work and humour.